How To Be Depressed

How To Be Depressed

George Scialabba

PENN

UNIVERSITY OF PENNSYLVANIA PRESS

Philadelphia

Published by
University of Pennsylvania Press
Philadelphia, Pennsylvania 19104-4112
www.upenn.edu/pennpress

Printed in the United States of America on acid-free paper
10 9 8 7 6 5 4 3 2 1

A Cataloging-in-Publication record is available from the Library of Congress.
ISBN 978-0-8122-5201-9

Contents

How To Be Depressed

I. Intake

Message from Room 101*

After reading George Orwell's *1984* in high school, I would sometimes wonder what was in Room 101. For each person, remember, it was whatever unhinged you, whatever you shuddered at most uncontrollably. "Everyone knows what is in Room 101," Winston Smith is told. "It is the worst thing in the world."

I was a fairly squeamish adolescent, so a good many possibilities suggested themselves, most of them with more than four legs. But I was also devoutly religious, and the hope of Heaven was of infinite comfort, limiting the horror of even the most lurid death. Now I no longer have that faith or that hope, and the question about Room 101 again seems a live one. I think I know the answer. The pain of a severe clinical depression is the worst thing in the world. To escape it, I would do anything. Like Winston, I would—at least I might—wish it on those I love, however dearly. But that's not feasible. The only way to escape it is to inflict my death on them. That is a grievous prospect, and I hope avoidable. But I know that those who do not avoid it cannot help themselves, any more than Winston could help betraying Julia.

Why? What is so unbearable about this pain? The primary sources are William Styron's *Darkness Visible*, Kay Jamison's *Unquiet Mind*, the "New York" section of Kate Millett's *The Loony-Bin Trip*, and the chapter "The Sick Soul" in William James's *Varieties of Religious Experience*. Others will someday improve on these accounts; I cannot. The

* The first chapter of *How To Be Depressed* was originally published in the literary magazine *Agni* in 2003.

most useful formulation is James's. Depression is "a positive and active anguish, a form of psychical neuralgia wholly unknown to normal life." Every word tells. "Positive and active": Acute depression does not feel like falling ill, it feels like being tortured. "Psychical neuralgia": The pain is not localized; it runs along every nerve, an unconsuming fire. In an agitated depression, my kind, it burns fiercely in the solar plexus and flares elsewhere, fed by obsessive fears, regrets, self-loathing. "Unknown to normal life": Because it feels unlimited in both intensity and duration, it truly is like no other pain. Even though one knows better, one cannot believe that it will ever end, or that anyone else has ever felt anything like it.

Certainty that an acute episode will last only a week, a month, even a year, would change everything. It would still be a ghastly ordeal, but the worst thing about it—the incessant yearning for death, the compulsion toward suicide—would drop away. But no, a limited depression, a depression with hope, is a contradiction. The experience of convulsive pain, along with the conviction that it will never end except in death— that is the definition of a severe depression. Commissar O'Brien tells Winston that the latter's dream of proletarian deliverance is a delusion, that his image of the future should instead be "a boot stamping on a human face—forever." The depressive's image of the future is "me, writhing in agony—forever." Flesh on an electrified grid; a dentist's drill tearing at an exposed nerve; a raging migraine; an implacable metastasis— but never ending.

How does this nightmare happen? Through an unlucky ratio of stress to strength, circumstance to constitution. The weaker one's nerves, the less it takes to inflame them. The more fragile one's neurochemical equilibria, the less it takes to disrupt them. How much you feel the daily slings and arrows depends on how thick your skin is.

Nature cuts most of us plenty of slack. "Most people," as Styron observes, "quietly endure the equivalent of injuries, declining careers, nasty book reviews, family illnesses. A vast majority of the survivors of Auschwitz have borne up fairly well. Bloody and bowed by the outrages of life, most human beings still stagger on down the road, unscathed by real depression." We are all issued neurological shock absorbers, usually good for a lifetime of emotional wear and tear. But if you're equipped with flimsy ones, or travel an especially rough road, the ride becomes very uncomfortable.

My shock absorbers seem to be exceptionally flimsy. Both of my parents were depressive: constantly worried, easily discouraged, with little capacity for enjoyment and no appetite for change. Except for a brief trip over the border of the next state to visit relatives, neither of them ever traveled more than fifty miles from where they were born. They were children during the Great Depression of the thirties, so during the Great Boom of the fifties and sixties and the Great Bubble of the eighties and nineties, they left their money—not that there was much of it; they were working-class people, conscientious but uneducated and unambitious—under the mattress or rolled up in the hollow legs of metal chairs. "Chronic severe dysthymia in a severely obsessional character" is my diagnosis and would have been theirs if they'd ever gotten one. It simply means "born to suffer."

Still, even with worn-out shock absorbers, life in a rich country is, at least some of the time, like a ride on a freshly paved road. Thanks to undemanding day jobs and a trickle of freelance income, I lived through the worst without institutionalization or destitution. So far. But old age looks grim. Chronic depression is very hard on lifetime earnings; and like many other people's, my retirement account is in trauma just now. In youth and middle age, one is supposed to store up material and psychic comfort against the years of decline. We all try to, but few people, healthy or ill, can fall back on as many resources as Styron, Jamison, or Millett. All three fully deserve their eminence, their affluence, their sympathetic friends and supportive families, their happy memories. And all, as their accounts make clear, would have died without those things. There is no doubt that good fortune is the best antidepressant.

But what about the unfamous, solitary, low-income depressed? We must suffer, and why shouldn't we? Life is unfair, after all. No talent, no distinction; no charms, no love. Natural enough: how else could admiration and affection, and the consolations they entail, possibly be distributed? Even to save a depressed person's life, you cannot admire or love him at will. In the trough of the illness, the sufferer's wheeze, shuffle, torpor, unvaryingly anguished expression, frequent humiliating flubs, and exasperating indecision rapidly exhaust any but the most heroic devotion. Few of us can claim such devotion.

Money is different, though. There is no natural way to apportion it. Some wealth, we all recognize, is unearned (quite a bit, if you go into the matter); and what is earned is not always deserved. No one can take credit for her own genetic endowment or early environment. Perfect markets do not and cannot exist. How we produce and distribute is a political question—economics is politics all the way down. Whether our current drastic inequality is fairer and more productive than our former moderate inequality depends entirely on what we're aiming to produce—and become.

People fall ill emotionally for any number of reasons, of course. As the poet Robert Lowell remarked, if we all had a little button on our forearm that we could press for a painless and instantaneous death, very few of us would reach old age. In some cases of severe depression, like mine, financial insecurity is central; in others, less so or not at all. There is always some way to help, and though nearly every way costs money, some would cost very little. Even a minimal government could afford them. Exercise, for example, is highly therapeutic for depression, but it is just what severely depressed people cannot force themselves to do. Young persons doing a year of national service could drag such people out for a vigorous walk each day, or do an hour of yoga with them. Or call them a few times a day to remind them to drink water—depressed persons nearly always dehydrate. Or drive them to a therapist—climbing the Himalayas is easier in some states of mind than getting out the front door is in others. The quantity of suffering diminished per dollar expended in these ways would be impressive.

Or you could give them money. As I slid into one episode, tormented by money worries, I saw an article by Robert Reich in the *American Prospect* magazine. He proposed exempting the first $20,000 of income from the payroll tax, the most regressive of all taxes. This would save 130 million American households an average of $5,000 per year. You could pay for this fully, he pointed out, by retaining the estate tax, the most progressive of all taxes, which affects only 2 percent of American households. Five thousand dollars a year would save a lot of ordinary people a lot of grief, and incidentally fix the economy. It might even save some lives.

Suicide, Albert Camus wrote, is the supreme philosophical problem. It is also, at least from the depressive's point of view, a political problem. The official figure for suicides in the United States is 30,000 annually, as of 2003, generally thought to be an understatement. Call it 40,000. I've read that two-thirds of these are severely depressed—say 25,000. Ten to fifteen percent of severely depressed people, it seems to be agreed, will eventually kill themselves. So—very, very approximately—each year 250,000 of your fellow citizens, one in nine hundred American adults, will be at risk of death from the protracted, indescribable pain of severe depression.

Reich's article mentioned that half of the estate tax, or around $350 billion, is paid by only 3,300 families. That's roughly one in 40,000 American households. If that money were simply handed over to the severely depressed, they would receive $1 million each. Bound to save some lives, though one should not underestimate the pain of lost Alpine ski vacations, designer clothes, and recreational drugs to the children of the superrich.

Also around this time, the philosopher John Rawls died. Everything is grist for one's obsessions, it's true; but the connection with Rawls is not really so far-fetched. Standing behind Rawls's famous veil of ignorance, you face a choice: You can accept one chance in 900 of being locked screaming in Room 101, together with one chance in 40,000 of avoiding all taxes on a huge estate. Or you can escape Room 101, and save many others from it, by giving up a negligible chance of enriching hypothetical heirs, not exorbitantly (that would still be permitted) but ultra-exorbitantly. Rawls would have thought the right choice obvious, and I suspect most Americans would agree with him, even if their elected representatives don't.

Admittedly, there are other, perhaps worthier, candidates for relief. Severe depression almost always ends, usually nonfatally. For many other people—a billion or so—illiteracy, malnutrition, diarrhea, infection, and other conditions far more easily preventable or curable than depression do not end. Even if these people's nerves are not on fire, Rawls might have judged theirs the more pressing claim. I think I could accept that judgment, even if for me it meant another spell in Room 101.

Why, you may be wondering, was this long whine ever written down? It's not a memoir, not an argument—what is it, anyway? The first draft—very much shorter and even purpler—was a suicide note, to be left behind on the riverbank or rooftop or night table. Emotional blackmail in a good cause, I told myself, though perhaps it was only spite, the feeble revenge of the ill on the well. In any case, I dithered. Like many other acutely depressed people I was, fortunately, too exhausted and disorganized to plan a suicide, much less compose an eloquent rebuke to an uncaring world. And then, very slowly, the fire died down. My viscera gradually unknotted, my energy seeped back, speech became less effortful, the world regained three dimensions. Blessedly, miraculously, everyday unhappiness returned.

Then why persist with the blackmail fantasy? Why risk bathos rather than keep a stoical and dignified silence? This was my third devastating depression, and probably not my last. I hope and intend to survive the coming ones, but already it seems urgent to try to salvage something from these ordeals. The conjunction of my pecuniary panic with a large-scale transfer of our national wealth to the already rich seemed to make an occasion. The vast popularity of depression memoirs and manuals in recent years suggests that there must be tens or hundreds of thousands of others whose sufferings, as intense as mine, would also have been lessened by crumbs of that wealth. And behind them, endless legions of the merely miserable. Perhaps they would want someone to say all this, however ineptly and futilely. If so, I won't have come back from hell empty-handed.

II. Documentia

My mental health file whirs to life in 1969 in Cambridge, Massachusetts. I'd recently left Opus Dei, the Catholic religious order to which I'd committed my young soul, and a major depression had followed. The records printed below are out of the mouths of my many caretakers; they chronicle my treatment at various medical offices and psychiatric clinics in the Boston area from then until 2016.

How did I come by them? As I headed into a depression a few years ago, a friend who was helping out thought it would be useful to see my records, so I asked for them. Why publish them now? Certainly not because I think these extracts from my treatment notes reveal an exceptionally interesting psyche, nor because I intend the slightest scandal to be visited on my therapists, employers, or insurance company. All proper names have been altered.

Then why foist on you these sad memorials of my four decades of depression? These medical records and treatment notes do not display any special literary facility. In fact, they're hardly written or composed at all—they're a very distinct form of writing, almost a form of anti-writing. Over the last thirty or forty years, the process of documenting such encounters has changed drastically. It used to be much more free-form, wide open, reflective, and candid. You can still see some of that here, but for the most part, as medical liability has become more of a concern and the whole society has become more litigious, providers have become very much more self-protective. Now, instead of employing an individual voice to portray an individual subject, they limit themselves to handing you expeditiously on to the next provider, the notes a sort of bill of lading.

Our distractible human intelligence needs as many ways of talking about depression as can be provided—that's all my motivation in publishing them. Given the longevity and tenacity of this particular demon in this particular life—mine—it seemed important to me to try to squeeze some insight from the mass of words and array of prescription drugs applied against its havoc. Even the most comprehensively bureaucratized medical knowledge can be made to speak, if only we are willing to listen closely to the blank spaces, the paraphrases, and even the acronyms.

The Crack-Up (1969–1970)

August 16, 1969
Trigg Clifton, MD/MB*
Harvard University Health Services, Psychiatric Clinic

Patient is seen as a courtesy visit because he is no longer actually eligible for consultation here, as he graduated here from the college [Harvard] in June of this year. He has plans to attend Columbia Graduate School.

He comes with very intense questions regarding Catholicism. In the last several months he has begun to question increasingly whether he can support a body of thought which stresses orthodoxy and lack of investigation. He approaches the problem with me and with himself quite intellectually, but he is indeed, in spite of intellect, feeling in much emotional turmoil over this. Support was given to him to move towards a middle ground, which, in his style, is very hard for him. He has felt frightened of the loss of the Church, and, therefore, it was clarified that he need not give up the Church, or the organization to which he belongs in the Church, to pursue his questioning, and that he would not be able to be content in any position he took until he opened up the questions with himself and others. He was also concerned that

---

* All proper names have been changed. For the sake of consistency and clarity, the formatting of certain elements has been standardized, such as dates and units of measurement. No substantive changes, however, have been made to the quoted material.

some of his actions have been inappropriate, and I did not feel that they were inappropriate save that they were indicative of a young man in considerable turmoil over some very important questions in life, and this was stated to the patient.

He will be talking with several priests and may indeed, when he gets to Columbia, seek psychiatric help for his semi-crippling obsessive-compulsive personality, i.e., he is often paralyzed by self-doubts and unable to be decisive.

At the end of the interview he questioned whether his difficulties would make him draft-deferrable. I stated that I did not think so.

Diagnoses: Adjustment Reaction of Adolescence in an obsessive-compulsive personality.

September 9, 1969
Trigg Clifton, MD/MB

Patient asked to be seen again because he now has to decide whether to go to Harvard Law School or to Columbia Graduate School. He spent the first fifty minutes of the session obsessing intellectually on both sides of the question, and I asked him very directly what his emotions told him, i.e. what he felt. He says that he now felt very uneasy about even the Church and Opus Dei. He felt that to pay attention to his emotions was a sign of weakness and lack of intellectual integrity. I clarified that man is both emotions and intellect, and it is lack of integrity not to be aware of the fact in making decisions. One must pay attention to one's intellect, although one does not necessarily obey what it says.

We worked further on the thought that Harvard Law School would be a somewhat more predictable school to be in, and that the more stable day-to-day life it would provide might allow him a base from which to (1) obtain psychotherapy with a lessening of day-to-day anxiety and (2) to allow him to think over his religious questions. Patient will consider these ideas, and if he does go to Harvard Law School will contact me regarding psychotherapy.

September 30, 1970
Trigg Clifton, MD/MB

The patient has been in New York City in graduate school at Columbia but had a severe obsessive breakdown in functioning, necessitating his dropping out of school. He was in treatment for about eight months in New York City but left two months ago, for reasons that are not clear. He is now back here, hoping to pull himself together, and plans to take courses through the Extension School.

He came to see me to reestablish contact, and to question if he could get into treatment. I am aware that his treatment has been difficult for him but see him as a very troubled man, and probably sicker than an adjustment reaction of adolescence—more likely borderline personality with obsessive-compulsive features. Obviously, he could not be treated at this clinic, and he is uncertain whether he wants to get into treatment at all. I told him that if he did, he should feel free to get in touch with me and I would find him a clinic in the area.

He is not suicidal, and there are no signs of acute decompensation.

A Season in Hell (1981)

August 17, 1981
Jennifer R. Hornstein, MD/MB
Harvard University Health Services, Psychiatric Clinic

This was the first Mental Health Service visit for this 33-year-old man, currently working as a receptionist for the Center for International Studies. He is a neatly groomed, articulate young man who has been suffering extreme anxiety for the past four months. Since April, he has had difficulty falling asleep, with midnight awakening and early morning awakening. Over the past few weeks he has only been able to sleep around five hours per night. He describes compulsive eating and heavy intake of "junk foods." He reports a loss of energy, anhedonia, and a decrease in sexual interest as well as a difficulty in obtaining erections. He denies suicidal or homicidal ideation. No history of hallucinations or delusions. No drug or alcohol use.

He says his current agitation reminds him of a period when he was 21, when he decided to leave a Catholic religious order which he had committed himself to, an order for laymen who dedicated themselves to chastity and poverty. Since then he has not been able to commit himself to any pursuits. Over the past several months, he has gone from one therapist to another, even including primal therapy. A therapist at the Harvard Community Health Plan prescribed some Valium, which helps him sleep but has not relieved his anxiety. Another therapist prescribed Sinequan, but it did not help.

Patient reports severe anxiety and obsessionality. He is unable to decide about anything, even whether to continue therapy. He is worried that there might be something medically wrong with him and has made an appointment to see his PCP [primary care physician]. He is not sure what he would like from me at this time, other than some instant relief or reassurance that his symptoms will not get much worse. He is afraid he will become so tired that he will not be able to walk across the campus to see me for our next appointment. I will see him Friday and then refer him for the two weeks that I am on vacation. He says he has friends who visit him occasionally, so he is not entirely isolated.

My initial impression is of a young man with agitated depression or anxiety attacks. No hyperventilation or palpitations but does describe some phobic symptoms (afraid he will stay in his house and not be able to leave). I do not think hospitalization is necessary. We discussed antidepressants, but I advised him that we would need further work-up before beginning medication.

August 21, 1981
Jennifer R. Hornstein, MD/MB

Mr. Scialabba returned for his second appointment. He appears slightly calmer than last time. His speech was slower and his affect more depressed. He describes a continuation of the symptoms noted on 8/17: difficulty falling asleep, early morning awakening, an urge to eat "junk food," difficulty making decisions, loss of energy, decrease in libido. He has frequent thoughts of dying and going to hell, which he connects with his experience in the Catholic Church.

He also appeared rather guarded when talking about a referral several years ago to the Homophile Community Health Service. He was referred to an individual who was a "good therapist." He denied that he had any thoughts about homosexuality or experience with homosexual liaisons.

He continued to demonstrate obsessive thought processes, though there were some loose associations, for instance when he began to quote from the gospel. Although the quotation was relevant to our discussion, his thinking did appear slightly tangential.

We continued to discuss his therapeutic history. He has had many experiences with therapists in the past, mostly short-term. After college he began therapy with Dr. Wendell O'Grady, a New York psychoanalyst, for six months. Shortly thereafter, he began treatment with the counselor at the Homophile Community Health Service. In the '70s he saw a therapist for one year, who was a member of SOMA [an alternative therapy collective]. In '71 he was in treatment for eight months as part of a group therapy with Alfred Lau. From '76 to '77 he was in an eight-month therapy which he describes as "scream therapy" with Raven McCracken at "Pathways." He saw Dr. Oliver Tipton in Cambridge for four sessions, the last appointment being four weeks ago. He saw Dr. Olliphant, a psychiatrist, on one occasion. She prescribed Sinequan of which he took 10 mgs. on one occasion.

My initial impression is that this is an agitated depression in a severely obsessional and schizoid young man. There is some question of whether he is decompensating to a psychotic state. There does seem to be some indication of intrusion of more primary process material. However, he appeared more organized (although more depressed) in this appointment than he had appeared on 8/17/81. This patient has had a physical examination with Dr. Cindy Shepard, his blood levels etc. are within normal limits.

My plan at this point is to order an EKG as well as a deximethasone suppression test. I gave the patient a prescription for 1 mg of Decadron to be taken at 11 p.m. on Sunday night and with instructions to have a 4 p.m. cortisol level drawn on Monday.

I discussed the possibility of psychological testing with Dr. Andrew Berl. In his estimation, it would be preferable to postpone psychological testing until after my vacation in early September. The reasons for this are twofold: first, if this is a decompensating process it would be helpful to observe the patient over the next two weeks; second, there is some possibility, although slight, that this psychological testing may make the patient more disorganized. This would be particularly difficult during my absence of the next two weeks. I would order psychological testing upon my return to consider the question of underlying psychotic process, to question issues of sexual identity, to evaluate depressive and suicidal ideation, to evaluate his reality testing, specifically around religious preoccupations, and to evaluate some of his ego strengths.

I have given the patient a prescription for Serax, with dosage instructions. He has taken Valium in the past without difficulty.

I would recommend that when he is seen next week the possibility of changing to an antipsychotic, such as Stelazine, be continued when he can be followed over the course of the week.

I have discussed this case with Dr. Jeffrey Parsnip, who will plan to see the patient on Wednesday at 3 p.m.

August 26, 1981
Jeffrey F. Parsnip, MD/MB
Harvard University Health Services, Psychiatric Clinic

As arranged by Dr. Jennifer R. Hornstein, I met with Mr. Scialabba today. My assessment, which is in agreement with Dr. Hornstein's, is that this man suffers from a rather severe endogenous depression superimposed on a schizoid personality.

Symptoms of major depression, which have been present for two to four months, include frequent early awakening; constipation; absent interest in sex; diurnal variations, with early morning the worst; compulsive eating; and profoundly decreased energy. I do not think that he suffers from true panic attacks but rather from somatic symptoms of anxiety.

The only family history of emotional illness is a first cousin, mother's brother's son, who committed suicide at age 21. There is no family history of alcohol abuse.

Certainly the chronic decline in functioning from his levels of a decade ago is disturbing. After graduating Harvard in 1969 with a group 2 average, he flunked out of Columbia, where he was studying history. Since then, he has spent a number of years working as a social worker in a local welfare department, though he says that this job was largely paperwork. He has been working as a receptionist at Harvard for the last year. He has no close friends and although he has had sexual intercourse he has not had close or enduring relationships.

He describes his mother as having been dominating, although very nervous, and his father as a timid, weak man. Father held an office job and mother worked in a textile factory. There is one brother who is taking night school courses and works in the Massachusetts Public Works Department. Thus, the patient greatly exceeded the level of the success of his family simply by going to Harvard and doing well there.

I wonder whether part of his subsequent decline is attributable to oedipal fears which his success represented. He now has multiple fears of losing control, which he fantasizes would result in his becoming passive, being unable to hold a job, going on welfare or into a hospital, and not being able to take care of himself. This may be a regression prompted by his earlier successes.

He describes having wanted to be a priest from the second or third grade, a role that was highly respected within his community. He currently has fears that his turning away from religion may have been a mistake and that he could be damned to hell for this. He also fears punishment for compulsive masturbation, which he says he is engaged in daily for ten years prior to his loss of sexual urges these last few months.

Given the chronic schizoid adaptation, the apparent decline in function over a ten-year period, and his interest in religion and philosophy, I looked hard for a thought disorder but was unable to satisfy myself of the presence of one. His functioning within the last four months is clearly discontinuous with his chronic level of functioning over the last ten years. During these four months he has had classic signs of an endogenous depression of severe degree, with agitation. In this context, I am rather strongly inclined to see him as having major depression superimposed on a schizoid personality.

Physical examination has been performed and is normal; dexamethasone suppression test is negative.

I believe he will likely benefit from tricyclic antidepressant therapy. I began discussing this with him today and will meet with him for further discussion tomorrow. Will probably start him on desipramine at that time.

September 14, 1981
Jennifer R. Hornstein, MD/MB

Mr. Scialabba's return appointment today. He has been on desipramine since August 27. States that he is lightheaded when he stands, also still lethargic and sedated. He saw Dr. Wolf before our appointment.

I spoke with Dr. Shepard, who informed me that he was postural. Blood pressure is indicated in the medical record.

Says he had a brief resurgence of energy at the end of August, but since then has had a resumption of his depressive symptoms. Broken sleep; appetite and sexual energy low. No signs of a thought disorder. Feels hopeless and helpless.

Summary of his medication is as follows: 8/27 desipramine 25 mg qhs. On 8/28—50 mg hs. From 8/29 until 8/30, 75 mg qhs. From 8/31 until 9/2, 100 mg qhs. From 9/4 until 9/7, he was on 150 mg desipramine. From 9/8 until 9/13, the dose was decreased 100 mg qhs for symptoms of faintness.

Given the patient's symptoms of faintness, lightheadedness, and postural hypotension, I have decreased his dose to 75 mg of desipramine. I will keep him on this dose for one week and then consider increasing the dose in slow increments.

I have discussed psychological testing with Maggie Ewing, who will refer him to a psychologist. I have requested that the psychological testing consider these questions: an underlying psychotic process, sexual identity, depressive and suicidal ideation, reality testing (specifically around religious preoccupations), and ego strengths.

The patient has stated that he is considering a referral to the Boston Center for Modern Psychoanalytic Studies. I have informed him that I will give him a referral if he wishes.

September 21, 1981
Jennifer R. Hornstein, MD/MB

Mr. Scialabba in for a return appointment. The medication is relieving his anxiety somewhat, but he continues to feel extremely sedated and exhausted. He has no further complaints or faintness or weakness. Still has some difficulty falling asleep, though not so much, and occasional early morning awakening. I increased his medication to 100 mgs of desipramine.

We discussed his frustration with his slow progress. He talked about his anger, and wondered whether it would be useful to spend the session expressing his anger. It seems he is particularly angry at the psychological evaluators who administered the psychological testing. He talked at great length about feeling insulted by the psychological test and expressed his anger at being dependent on "clerks and stupid bureaucrats." He associated this with more longstanding anger at feeling dependent upon his mother, whom he also saw as a kind bureaucrat, and as vindictive and unavailable. In contrast he said he felt close to his father, a civil engineer.

He continued, affirming his anger at having to depend upon incompetent people, and at the same time acknowledged his very strong wish to be taken care of. He felt this particularly strongly in our sessions and wished I could see him more often. He could not articulate what he had hoped to gain by meeting more often, other than a sense that he was being looked after.

His affect was alternately sad and angry. He started to cry at one point, talking about his own compassion for suffering people and his wish that his own suffering would be treated with similar compassion.

September 28, 1981
Jennifer R. Hornstein, MD/MB

Mr. Scialabba appeared slightly more energetic and less fatigued than previously. He continues angry and frustrated with the psychological evaluation, and with bureaucracy in general.

He went on to speak about a longstanding sense of frustration, dating back at least to the age of 21. Again he spoke now of a strong wish to be taken care of, as well as frustration that he was not getting immediate relief from the medication. Despite that frustration, he appeared notably more animated today.

October 5, 1981
Jennifer R. Hornstein, MD/MB

He appears much improved today: more alert and articulate, less angry and agitated. His sleep has improved and he feels less anxious. He attributed this in part to the medication and in part to his article being accepted for publication by the *Village Voice*. During today's session the change in his presentation was noticeable. He was less argumentative and more thoughtful. He was more obsessional than usual but less tearful and distracted. He spoke of the significance of his becoming 33. He felt that this age marked the end of early adulthood and meant he could no longer fall back on the fact that he was young, but had to begin to consider why he had not achieved more to date.

He wonders whether he should return to primal scream therapy and whether his current episode may have been related to early childhood experiences. In particular, he described a sense of frustration of not being taken care of as he would have liked by his mother. He fears that such concerns would not be taken seriously in other forms of therapy.

Mr. Scialabba appears to be coping with his anxiety with more obsessional defenses at this point. He appears more available for therapy at this time.

October 19, 1981
Jennifer R. Hornstein, MD/MB

Mr. Scialabba appeared calm and in good spirits today. He has felt quite confident since his article appeared. He also attributes some of the improvement to the medication. We discussed some of the results of the psychological testing.

In answer to his question about primal therapy, I suggested that he embark on a weekly course of psychotherapy, probably long term. I told him that his difficulty was not in experiencing affect, but rather in integrating his feelings with his intellectual perceptions. When he begins to experience feelings, he feels overwhelmed, panicked, and becomes frightened. When writing, on the other hand, uses his intellectual capacity exclusively. It appears that the task will be to help integrate both the intellectual and the affective experiences. I referred him to Dr. James Garcia, for possible therapy.

November 17, 1981
Jennifer R. Hornstein, MD/MB

Mr. Scialabba has decided not to continue with Dr. James Garcia. There is apparently some financial difficulty. He has decided instead to meet in once-a-week therapy with Dr. Buenavista through the Boston Center for Modern Psychoanalysis. I have suggested that he ask whether he could receive the medication through the Boston Center for Modern Psychoanalysis or through a physician associated with the Center. I have advised him quite strongly that I see difficulties in splitting up the therapy from the medication in his case. He will get back to me next week about this.

He seems in good spirits today. He is calm, less anxious, and reports that he is sleeping six to seven hours a day. His appetite is good. He has more energy and is attending work without difficulty. No crying episodes. He has occasional headaches—every two or three weeks. Other than this, no medication-related side effects. I renewed his prescription for desipramine and advised him to increase his fluid intake since his last BUN was 20.

Reality Components (1986–1987)

December 29, 1986
Grace Franklin, MD/MTL
McLean Hospital

Of his background I learned that he is the younger of two children born to second-generation Italian parents. Although he speaks kindly and sensitively about his parents, he describes his home life as deprived in some ways, based on his parents' educational and socio-economic status. Very difficult relationship with his mother, who was highly critical and demanding and who could not be pleased. He has a good relationship with his only sibling, a brother who lives in the area, is married with children, and works in the same city department for which his father worked for twenty or thirty years. He feels somewhat estranged from his family because he broke away intellectually and educationally, but nonetheless sees them on a regular basis every three or four weeks and the relationship is cordial.

As we talked about what he is seeking in therapy, it came out that he has a good deal of intellectual insight. Indeed his major defenses are intellectual and rather powerful. He defends against affect and he defends against intimacy; I suspect this is the reason his therapy has not gotten very far in the past. Indeed, his relationships with therapists haven't gone much further than his relationship with anyone else in his life. When we began to talk about his wishes regarding a therapist, the resistances immediately surfaced. Money is a problem for him: his insurance coverage is not good, and while he does have some small savings, he is not sure at this point how much he wants to commit his savings to treatment. This clearly is not going to be an easy treatment situation, although I think he would be a very interesting person to work with. I think he should be in the hands of a very experienced therapist, someone well trained in developmental issues. There's an additional factor: this man has had two major periods of upheaval in his life, and although the history is not clear-cut, I found myself thinking in terms of a possible recurrent depression. At one point in 1980, when he was seen at UHS [University Health Service], he was put on an antidepressant. He cannot tell me whether his depression responded to the antidepressant or just went away spontaneously. His mother seems to have a great deal of emotional difficulty, and there was a cousin on the mother's side who committed suicide, so there is a possible biochemical or genetic vulnerability. For this reason, I feel that he also ought to be in the hands of a physician who will be sensitive to medical issues. In short, in this one session, the diagnosis is not clear. This is a man with a narcissistic character; a manic-depressive diagnosis must be ruled out. Because he could not make up his mind today about treatment and could not advise me how to refer him it was left that he will consider his assets, get more information about his insurance, and when he is ready to be referred he will be in touch with me so that I can be more helpful to him.

February 1987
Grace Franklin, MD/MTL

Mr. Scialabba remains ambivalent about therapy. He couches it in terms of his inability to afford any ongoing treatment, and I do think that is partly realistic. He asked whether Valium on a regular basis might be useful. As we discussed this, he mentioned an article by a prominent writer about using Valium for symptoms not unlike his. Unfortunately, she became a Valium addict, so Mr. Scialabba in effect answered his own question. I reaffirmed my views that many of the things he was coping with were characterological, and that was not an indication for Valium use. We did talk a bit about anti-depressants, whether they had a role in his treatment. Since I saw him last, he's had two periods of depression, which were very short-lived, generally just a couple of days, and most of the time he's been feeling fairly well. I don't have enough of the indications myself to put him on anti-depressant, but I told him that I was fairly conservative about the use of drugs and encouraged him, if he wished, to have a consultation with a psycho-pharmacologist to see whether someone with this kind of experience might recommend the use of them. I gave him the names of Douglas Ore, Tom Elfwood and Robert Ellis as possible consultants to this end.

Mr. Scialabba is a 38-year-old Harvard employee, who comes to me for a referral for ongoing therapy. He's a graduate of Harvard College, class of '69, has had a fair amount of treatment with a variety of therapists in the past, including having been seen by a number of people in the UHS, although that record was not available to me today. He recognizes that he is stalemated in his life and his career and that it's emotional problems that are blocking him from taking next developmental step. He wants to definitively go to work on these problems. Though he's seen many therapists in the past and has made some progress with some and with others considered the experience worthless, he has never been able to grow in the way he clearly needs to do if he's going to move beyond his current position. By that he means that he has considerable intellectual capability, was originally planning to go into a religious order but split off from that when he was in college, did begin graduate school at Columbia but was in so much emotional turmoil and was unable to concentrate that even that came to an end after a year. Since that time he has had a variety of low-level jobs and although he functions adequately in them, he is certainly not living up to his intellectual potential at all. This is also true in his personal life, he lives alone, he has some friends, but he only allows people to get so close to him. His best friend is an old one from the past but one who lives in New York, and I gather the friendship is expressed mostly by letter. There have been many women in his life but the relationships have always been short-lived, and when he begins to sense that the woman wants to go further with the relationship, he begins to find things that are wrong and creates such distance that the relationship breaks off.

April 13, 1987
Grace Franklin, MD/MTL

In case he changes his mind about ongoing therapy, I gave him Margaret Williams's name. Her clinic might be able to offer him a reduced fee for therapy that would be manageable for him.

Intermittently Hopeless (1987–1988)

July 6, 1987
Melinda R. Maron
McLean Hospital, Ambulatory Care Services

Intake Report

Chief Complaint:

Patient saw Dr. Mason once. Referred him here because of financial concerns. Feels emotionally fragile, high-strung, unable to make life decisions. Feels he's drifting professionally. "Ridiculously over-qualified for what he does."

History of Present Problem:

Early traumatic break from religious tradition, Catholicism, at age 21 from which he's never really recovered.

Family Information/Current Living Situation:

Lives alone. Parents and one brother live in the area.

Medical History/Current Medications:

Physically in good health, though not "bursting with energy."
No meds, alcohol or drugs.

Previous Outpatient Treatment:

Yes—few times in the '70s.

Previous Hospitalizations:

None.

Additional Psychiatric History:

One cousin had psych problems and suicide at age 22.

Insurance Coverage:

Harvard University Group Health Plan (HUGHP)

Impression at Intake:

Patient found it difficult to talk, seemed very constricted and upset.

August 25, 1987
Juan Durendal, MD
McLean Hospital, Ambulatory Care Services

S. I was feeling really down when I called you.
O. Anxious, mildly depressed, ruminative.
A. Given history of anxiety with prominent somatic components, depression, following relatively minor negative events, n/o phobias, an MAOI seems indicated. Patient aware of risks and benefits of trial, understands possibility of HTN [hypertensive response] if not following

diet. Aware of the need for concomitant psychotherapy, agrees to see Melinda Maron weekly.

P. 1) Start Parnate 10 mg po. Follow-up in a week.

August 25, 1987
Juan Durendal

S. I'm intermittently hopeless.

O. Very tense, restless, sighing, unchanged from previous meetings. Patient had to turn down a teaching job offered to him by a friend because of overwhelming anxiety, fear of failure or "crack-up." Felt better after turning it down but became somewhat hopeless. No side effects from Parnate.

Increase Parnate to 20 mg. Follow-up in a week.

September 9, 1987
Juan Durendal

S. Feeling the same, sleeping more or less okay.

O. Tense, anxious still ruminating about giving up the opportunity to teach history because of his anxiety.

A/P. Tolerating increasing doses of Parnate, no side-effects prominent.

Increase Parnate to 30 mg po AM. Follow-up in a week.

September 23, 1987
Juan Durendal

S. I've been having some orthostatic hypotension, my mood is as usual.

Constricted, anxious affect. Sleeping well, waking up once during the night as is usual for him, well rested in the morning. Patient is interested in shifting his sleeping pattern from sleeping between 2:00 a.m.—10:00 a.m. to something like 12:00 midnight—7:00 a.m. to be able to have a more socially active life, prepare papers for courses, etc.

A. Tolerating Parnate 40 mg d, some orthostatic hypotension, some increased energy. Finds therapy to be beneficial "at least I have someone intelligent to talk to." Will attempt shifting his s/a cycle over the next 2–3 wks. Patient given instructions regarding hygienic measures to improve sleep. Will discuss starting cognitive Rx.

P. Continue Parnate 40 mg Halcion 0.123 mg for insomnia.

December 3, 1987
Melinda R. Maron

Met with Mr. Scialabba for 50 minutes. Focus of session was his difficulties in relationships; feeling either intimidated and unequal or feeling superior and condescending. Pattern is to avoid all relationships. Lately, however, is making attempts to socialize.

December 10, 1987
Melinda R. Maron

Said that for him the pursuit of pleasure and self-expression seems to be confused with anger. Said a woman in a psychotherapy group once described him as a "ticking bomb." He feels that in some way this is true. Is afraid of his angry impulses. Feels he has to "pay his dues" by paying attention to politics and taking moral stands. Worries he left Opus Dei for pursuit of pleasure rather than on principle. Very conflicted regarding both pleasure and regression.

December 17, 1987
Melinda R. Maron

Patient talked about his difficulty with intimate relationships. Feels he can only succeed with young, naïve women, who won't perceive his failings. A "mature" relationship with a "mature" woman is something he avoids. Mr. S seems to worry about every aspect of relationships. Also ambivalent about gratifying his more "superficial" impulses.

December 24, 1987
Melinda R. Maron

Patient reports some old obsessions coming back now. He is again envious of friends and feeling inferior to them. Described his wish to be a reclusive mouse of an academic who would bury himself in serious academic work rather than being the "dabbler" he feels himself to be. Worries that he's superficial because won't allow himself to pursue literature and philosophy, which is what he wants to do. Near the end of the session, he described a scene from adolescence when he tried to resolve a conflict on the playground between "good" boys and "tough" boys.

December 30, 1987
Melinda R. Maron

Treatment Plan

Problem No. 1:

Depression as shown by social isolation, inability to make career decisions, and overwhelming feelings of guilt.

Goal (long term):

Reduce feelings of guilt, paralysis about decision, and social isolation.

Objectives (short term):

Patient will understand more about the connection between his behavior and his depression, and will feel less despair and guilt about his choices.

Expected Achievement Dates:

Long term—6/90
Short term—9/88

Specific Plans:

Individual psychotherapy, once per week.
Psychopharmacology with behavior therapy, once per month.

Problem No. 2:

Personality disorder with obsessive-compulsive style and depression that contribute to his paralysis and lack of intimate relationships.

Goal (long term):

Modification of obsessive-compulsive defenses.

Objectives (short term):

Patient will become more flexible and tolerant of himself and his affects.

Expected Achievement Dates:

Long-term—6/90
Short-term—9/88

Termination Criteria:

Reduce depression. Modification of rigidity of obsessive-compulsive personality disorder.

Chief Complaint:

Mr. Scialabba described himself as "emotionally fragile, high-strung, and unable to make life decisions. I am ridiculously over-qualified for what I do; I feel stalled in my life and want to know if there is a medication that could help me."

<u>History of Presenting Problem:</u>

Mr. Scialabba dates his psychiatric symptoms back to age 14, when he developed incapacitating anxiety in response to any sexual impulse, along with guilty ruminations that disrupted his usual activities. He went to a priest who told him he would take responsibility before God for the patient's sexual impulses, and the anxiety episodes stopped.

Some years later, he joined a very devout all-male Catholic organization called Opus Dei and was very involved with that organization during his undergraduate years at Harvard. He felt a missionary zeal about attracting others to Opus Dei. He describes his commitment as "intense, demanding, and lifelong." But after four years of college he "lost all belief in Catholicism."

Mr. Scialabba describes his leaving the Catholic Church and Opus Dei as extremely difficult. He went into a meeting of Opus Dei and tried to speak publicly about his loss of faith. Instead he became so agitated that had to be led from the room. He feels he has never recovered from this emotional upset. He describes the time leading up to his departure from Opus Dei as the most intensely meaningful, exciting time in his life, when he felt that all of life and intellectual and philosophical pursuits were open to him. Instead when he left, he was overwhelmed by agitation.

He attempted graduate school at Columbia in European intellectual history as well as Harvard Law School, but he dropped out of both because whenever he attempted to do any serious work, he would become unbearably agitated and have to stop. He returned to Cambridge after one year at Columbia and has remained here ever since.

Mr. Scialabba has had a series of "undemanding and rewarding jobs" such as substitute teaching, welfare social worker, and currently is a receptionist/staff assistant at Harvard's Center for International Studies. During the last 5 years he has done a fair amount of freelance book reviewing for the *Village Voice*, the *Boston* Phoenix, and a journal called *Grand Street*.

January 7, 1988
Melinda R. Maron

Talked about commitment. He described himself as "butter-fly-like," floating from one thing to another without ever really choosing. Feels this has been his pattern in life—he doesn't want to give up anything. When you choose, you are left with paralyzing doubts, as he was after leaving Opus Dei.

January 7, 1988
Juan Durendal

S: "I am feeling discouraged again. This time of year always gets me down because it reminds me how little I've accomplished in the last year."

O: Mental status exam essentially unchanged. No side effects from Parnate.

A: We have started doing behavior therapy focusing on vocational and interpersonal issues. No change in meds appears warranted, although tolerance to Parnate is possible. Will continue to observe.

January 12, 1988
Melinda R. Maron

About 5 years ago Mr. Scialabba experienced an episode of major depression with low mood, decreased concentration, initial insomnia, decreased appetite, decreased energy, moderate anhedonia, social isolation, guilty ruminations and wishes of being dead, but with no suicidal ideation. The stressor was the need to either to buy the apartment in which he lived or to vacate it. Mr. Scialabba improved spontaneously in September. He ended up buying the apartment with the help of his family.

Recently Mr. Scialabba again became depressed during the summer months with no obvious stressor. He began to feel very stuck in his life and wanted to do something about it, and that prompted his seeking treatment.

Personal History:

Mr. Scialabba grew up in East Boston in an Italian Catholic working-class family. He has one brother, with whom he has a somewhat distant relationship. He describes his mother as a strict powerful figure in his childhood, who was angry and bitter about her working-class status and disappointed in her husband for not being ambitious enough. Mr. Scialabba recalls his father as being passive and dominated by his mother. He also felt afraid of his mother's anger, although he does not remember her as being abusive. He was a quiet, sensitive, "good" child who always wanted to please the nuns at school, where he always did very well. He felt somewhat isolated and yearned to escape his East Boston neighborhood. He reports nothing remarkable during his childhood or adolescence until age 14 when he briefly developed anxiety around his sexual impulses. He visits his parents in East Boston several times a month.

The patient has never had any drug or alcohol problems. He seldom has a drink. He has had several casual sexual relationships with women, but none have become serious involvements. Mr. Scialabba states that his "incapacity for intimacy seems overdetermined: first, by a lack of professional achievement, stability or status; and second, because I am so excruciatingly high-strung." He feels he is emotionally immature, both because of his difficulties with intimacy and because having children seems unimaginable.

Mr. Scialabba also reports that though he was a "healthy, energetic adolescent," he is now "physically, delicate: I lie in bed late, wear pajamas around the house, sensitive to cold." He stays up late nights, rising late in the morning.

Presently Mr. Scialabba has a number of male friends, writers and intellectuals with whom he constantly compares himself and to whom he feels inferior. He had opportunities to teach freshman English at Boston University and at Boston College this year, but was so anxious and agitated at the prospect that he declined. He felt that this disappointed his friends greatly, and certainly disappointed himself.

Mr. Scialabba describes himself as a "dabbler" in intellectual history and politics who can impress people superficially but is lacking in depth, because he could not commit himself intellectually any more than he could emotionally.

He thinks that some of his problems have to do with an incapacity to say no—he "certainly had trouble saying no to Opus Dei." He suspects he has a great deal of "repressed anger" which has led to his present "emotional paralysis."

Previous Psychiatric History:

Mr. Scialabba has tried psychotherapy several times before but has given it up because of "lack of success or money." He sought treatment in the mid-1970s without any relief of symptoms. In 1981, he had a clinical depression and was seen at Harvard University Health Services, where it was thought that his depression was biochemically induced and he was prescribed desipramine. Soon afterward, his depression improved. Presently Mr. Scialabba is also being seen by Dr. Juan Durendal for psychopharmacology. He is taking Parnate for treatment of generalized anxiety and dysthymic disorder as well as being seen in individual psychotherapy one time weekly.

Mental Status:

Mr. Scialabba is an attractive, well-groomed, conservatively dressed man. He is exceedingly thin and of average height, angular, with dark eyes and dark, curly hair. He makes good eye contact, is cooperative and pleasant but tense and controlled. His mood is described as "nervous and sometimes overwhelmed." His affect is constricted, tending toward the serious, but also anxious and depressed. He reports having difficulty with anger and rarely expresses sadness. He claims to be flirtatious and seductive with women and has a propensity for allusion and word play. His speech is logical; he speaks in full sentences with a wide vocabulary. Often, however, he will become verbally entangled and halting as he tries to explain himself with obsessional accuracy. There are some feelings of envy and jealousy and some guilty ruminations which are quite self-punitive. No disorders of perception, cognition, or orientation. Intelligence above average. His memory is intact, but early memories regarding himself and his family are vague. Judgment and capacity for intellectual insight are good, but the underlying affect appears unavailable because of various rigid defenses: rationalization, obsessiveness, intellectualization, and somatization. Self-estimation alternates between harsh self-criticism and timid grandiosity.

Course of Interviews:

Mr. Scialabba arrives consistently and on time for once per week 50-minute individual psychotherapy. He has had a great deal of difficulty with morning appointments, even as late as 9:00 o'clock. Initially Mr. Scialabba talked at length about his anxieties around taking a teaching job which he ultimately declined because of his fears of failure and because of the pressure it would put on him, interfering with his ability to pursue his real interests in intellectual history and writing. Mr. Scialabba talked at length about his paralysis around career decisions and his tendency to stay in a job that makes few demands on him.

Gradually he has begun to talk somewhat more personally about issues of intimacy, sexuality, and aggression. He became less depressed quite soon in the treatment. He went on to speak of a writing assignment. He became very reclusive and avoided friends to work on the review most of the time. He admitted that he has a great deal of difficulty altering his routines and feels terrible if he doesn't read the many periodicals he subscribes.

When Mr. Scialabba finished his book review, he again began to be preoccupied with the themes that depress him, particularly the problem of where he is headed in his career. He also ruminates about his relationships with women and feels that he tends to get into superficial relationships in the same way he tends to "dabble" in many intellectual areas instead of focusing on one. He is indecisive about returning to graduate school. He began two courses this fall with that in mind but gave them up to work on his review.

In general Mr. Scialabba expressed anxiety and conflict around activity/passivity and around his aggressive and sexual impulses. He describes his sexual fantasies as having elements of domination and aggression in them and feels ashamed of this. If he actively pursues his interest in literature and philosophy, he feels guilty and is compelled to continue writing about politics because that is the socially admirable thing to do and does not involve the pursuit of his own pleasure.

Mr. Scialabba expresses positive feelings about his therapy but pursues it in a highly logical and intellectualized style. He became quite distraught at one point when he felt there was a significant disagreement between him and the therapist. He expressed his belief in primal therapy and catharsis, and the therapist did not embrace these. At this point it seems evident that the transference relationship cannot tolerate much anger or disillusionment. He clearly wants to protect the relationship, and he's curious as to why he looks forward to coming. For now he uses treatment to intellectually pursue a resolution to what he calls his "neurosis." Attempts to soften or respond neutrally to his harsh self-criticism are tricky for the therapist. On the one hand he wants to be liked, but on the other hand he thrives on intellectual vigor and tends to see non-criticalness as intellectual weakness. If he allows a different perspective about himself and his motivation some meaning, as he has begun to do in treatment, he will be able to become more flexible in his relationships.

Formulation:

Mr. Scialabba is a 40-year-old single white male with an Italian Catholic upbringing that was both rigid and intense. In childhood and adolescence he excelled academically and described himself as a compliant, well-behaved boy, exceedingly devoted to his religion. He describes no adolescent upheaval or rebellion and in fact managed his sexual impulses by turning to the Church with more tenacity and by becoming "dependent on the structure of Opus Dei for his identity." After four years of college at Harvard and four years of intense conformity and austere commitment to Opus Dei, he found himself full of religious doubt and very excited about following his intellectual pursuits. He left Opus Dei with much difficulty and nagging guilt that he had made the wrong decision and had done this for motives which included the pursuit of sexual gratification. Since that time Mr. Scialabba has found himself unable to function appropriately academically and professionally, especially given his strengths. He feels arrested emotionally and developmentally. In fact, serious developmental arrests do seem to have occurred in his capacity to express and to modulate affects, in the management of his aggression and sexuality, and in the capacity for relatedness and intimacy with other people. His superego development is extremely harsh and punitive, and he has never adequately formed an identity he can feel comfortable with. He is often in conflict and paralyzed by it, and he has developed rigid defenses, particularly intellectualization, as well as obsessive and phobic traits which perpetuate his social and professional isolation. Mr. Scialabba has also had several major depressive episodes in his life which appear to have a biological component as well as intrapsychic and developmental components. His most recent depression has no obvious external precipitant, but he was about to turn 40 and felt his life had been on hold for nearly 20 years. His self-esteem suffers severely during these depressions—he compares himself negatively with his friends and experiences their successes as narcissistic injuries to himself.

Mr. Scialabba is a very bright man who can be engaging, witty, and conversational. He has a capacity for insight but relies so extremely on intellectualization that very little affect is available for genuine insight. He is quite introspective and curious about himself and others, although ultimately highly critical and perfectionistic. He is hopeful and interested in his therapy but disillusionment with his therapist will be a difficult adjustment for him.

Treatment Formulation:

Mr. Scialabba will be seen for psychopharmacology by Dr. Juan Durendal for treatment of his recent major depression. He will be seen weekly in individual psychotherapy for his obsessive-compulsive personality disorder, which is contributing to his professional paralysis, his inability to form a lasting, intimate relationship, and his self-punitive, inflexible sense of guilt. Long-term goals include modification of Mr. Scialabba's rigidly intellectualized defensive structure, allowing for more relatedness and more affect, some relenting of his harsh self-criticism, and an improved capacity to make decisions in his professional and personal life. Success depends on developing a positive transference that can tolerate the anger, frustration, and devaluation that inevitably will come.

January 14, 1988
Melinda R. Maron

Talked about his Italian East Boston background. He worries that if he let himself, he'd regress back to being like his parents, sentimental and emotional. Reads me a passage from Henry James about the moral defects of the Italian character. Feels he's "full of his race." Says he tries to isolate the emotional side of himself for fear that all "20 years of Cambridge sophistication" would be lost. Mr. S. was 5 minutes late and very upset about it. Worried that therapist would see it as hostile rejecting resistance.

January 28, 1988
Melinda R. Maron

Talked about his shame at being in his current position and inability to see his writing accomplishments as real aspects of his identity.

"You are what you're paid to do." Wishes he could simply wake up and feel like going out in the world to get a new job. Patient also talked about cowlick in hair (very proud of his hair) and falling asleep early in the evening.

February 11, 1988
Melinda R. Maron

Mr. Scialabba spoke of an incident that may have precipitated his last depression. He was having long and difficult dental work done and when he found the dentist unsympathetic with his pain, he abruptly terminated the dental work which he now regrets. He associated the relationship with his mother and longing to be nurtured and cared for. He is beginning to feel some of this in the transference, though he claims not to understand what he is feeling.

February 19, 1988
Melinda R. Maron

He reports feeling depressed and "fretful" over the weekend because of the successes of two friends, which made him feel like a failure. We talked about identity issues, his future as a writer, and his low-self-esteem connected with his job as a receptionist. But feels very anxious when he thinks of leaving security of job.

February 23, 1988
Melinda R. Maron

Talked about why he cannot accept his way of life right now. Then talked about difficulty in relationships with women. Said all his sexual relationships seem to assume the character of foreplay, and he wasn't altogether certain how he felt about that.

The Madonna and the Whore (1988–1991)

March 10, 1988
Melinda R. Maron
McLean Hospital, Ambulatory Care Services

Patient recovering from being sick. Talked about having some positive feelings about his writing and acknowledged that he is a writer with some "small" talent. Talked about worries that Dr. Durendal may have given up on him because he's been unable to move ahead on goals they set. Got into a discussion about his concern that his helpless feelings and need for acceptance will drive therapists away. Worries his needs are limitless.

March 17, 1988
Melinda R. Maron

Patient came in eager to tell me about a dream in which he'd gotten very angry with his father and in "self-defense" threatened to "beat the shit out of him." Felt this was a very unusual dream for him, since he never expresses anger. Talked at length about his relationship with his parents. Takes pleasure in arguing with father but can never convince his mother, which is very frustrating. Feels mother has "worn him down," though he feels triumphant whenever she expresses a liberal view. Described mother as hysterical, emotionally fragile, and the emotional center of family.

March 24, 1988
Melinda R. Maron

Patient recently met a woman he "fell immediately in love with." Asked therapist to give him advice on how to tell a woman editor he's involved with that he is in love with this new woman. Patient didn't seem to feel much sense of impulsivity of this new "love."

March 31, 1988
Melinda R. Maron

He begins by saying he is "in love," but is also anxious, worried that catastrophe is imminent. He said he always thought that he wasn't a person for whom a relationship would be very important. Always thought he would be alone—as an adolescent he thought he would become a priest. Also, he remembers his depression of 4 years ago and wonders if he's too emotionally fragile to be able to manage a relationship. He recalled a period in his adolescence when he became extremely agitated because he kept having "impure" thoughts, often sexual thoughts (he'd see male and female genitals symbolically). He went to priest who was very non-punitive and told him not to worry about the thoughts because the priest would be responsible for them. In college his sexuality was very sublimated, with highly charged, excited reactions to things he read. Recalled falling in love with George Eliot because her soul was so beautiful. He was lying on the floor one night praying when a picture of George Eliot (a photo he'd seen of her with light radiating behind her face), came to mind along, with feelings of love. Thought he might one day fall in love with a woman with some of George Eliot's qualities. Mr. S. said Opus Dei saw marriage as weakness (for the "troops" not for the "officers" of God's army). Mr. S. reported beginning to masturbate after leaving Opus Dei. (During adolescence he would not touch himself because that was sinful and thought of orgasm as an accident.) He sensed disapproval from mother about his few masturbating experiences. When Mr. S. was so agitated during adolescence, his parents suggested he sleep one night with his father.

Mr. S says his masturbatory fantasies now are always with a woman whom he doesn't care about, one he can control and dominate. When he slept with the woman this weekend whom he's falling in love with, he couldn't get erect at first, because he cared too much about her. Mr.

S. called this his "Madonna/Whore" split. Talked about how important the split had been when ideal love was associated with God and sexuality was sinful and something to be repressed or denied. Very difficult for him to integrate the two now.

April 7, 1988
Melinda R. Maron

Patient came in reporting that his new relationship is going well, but old feelings are beginning to come up again, like feeling he does not have enough time to spend with her. Still concerned about whether he cannot have a successful relationship because he is "too fragile."

April 17, 1988
Melinda R. Maron

Relationship still going well. Thinks it could become a long-term relationship but fears he could "freeze up" again and that would end it. Talked about how he has gotten out of commitments in the past by making himself appear emotionally weak and fragile.

April 21, 1988
Melinda R. Maron

Mr. S. talked about his tendency to notice defects in any woman he's involved with. Says he's always associated getting married with being trapped: fear that a woman changes after she gets a man and becomes controlling and demanding and nagging as his mother was with his father. Identifies with his father's passivity and lack of ambition, which his mother criticized. Patient seems to carry his parents' struggle about this inside himself and nags himself for being like his father. Wonders if his perfectionism is his way of escaping becoming like his parents. Talked about feeling of connectedness with therapist, like an infant wanting to be taken care of but nevertheless doesn't feel dependent. Confused by the feeling.

May 5, 1988
Melinda R. Maron

Patient reported incident with mother, who after periods of being aloof and critical would ask him "Who is the best boy in the world? Who loves you the most?" Patient used to feel resentful about having to respond to this and felt he could not respond honestly or genuinely. Explored conflicts around activity and passivity.

May 19, 1988
Melinda R. Maron

Patient worried that he isn't getting enough work done and that the relationship he is in distracts him from work. Wonders if he'll ever be able to tolerate being close to anyone.

May 26, 1988
Melinda R. Maron

Patient worries that he isn't working hard enough between sessions (i.e. he hasn't been thinking about what we've talked about and even has trouble remembering a week later). It became apparent, however, that Mr. Scialabba had followed through on applying for a job we had discussed (although the job may not now be available) and that he was feeling less critical of himself and more relaxed after our sessions. Explored the thought that perhaps his "homework" was to *not* work so hard at critically analyzing himself.

June 10, 1988
Melinda R. Maron

Mr. S recorded having a "fantastic" week yet feels there is still "something missing," that he is cut off from his emotions ("an iceberg underneath"). Feels he is not "whole." Talked at length about fears of losing control emotionally and was able to relate this to the overpowering fear he had as a child of saying "no" to God. Mr. S appeared very moved by this association. Wondered if he would ever be able to "say no to God."

June 16, 1988
Melinda R. Maron

Mr. S 5 minutes late and somewhat agitated about it. Frustrated this week because he hasn't been able to finish an important book review on time. Fears he is going to be chastised, even though he knows this won't happen. Discussed ways in which Mr. S takes frustration out on himself and even undermines his own goals.

June 23, 1988
Melinda R. Maron

Mr. S wanted to talk about dream in which he was visiting a family (he compared it to William F. Buckley's family), which he did (in the dream) once a year and felt something erotic for both the mother and a young adolescent girl who was also visiting the family. As the dream evolves the adolescent girl kills herself and Mr. S feels responsible in some ill-defined way, although there is another "unsavory" character in the dream who seems to share some responsibility. Discussion of the dream led to discussion of how he might integrate a more loving attitude towards his naïve (fragile) innocent self and his more "unsavory and worldly" aspects. Suggested he attempt to work on a more benign view of himself and his impulses, especially his sexual impulses.

June 30, 1988
Melinda R. Maron

Patient again brought dream to session, which led to discussion of his relationship with his mother. Explored the process of separating from a very controlling mother and accompanying issues of the betrayal and disloyalty. Patient moves from a position of being cowardly in his dream to being courageous and fighting back. He relates to having more hope in his life because of his relationship with Ellen and because of his therapy.

July 19, 1988
Melinda R. Maron

Patient reported having had a fine vacation. Says he is not as depressed this summer as he expected to be because of the therapy and because of his relationship with Ellen. Patient talked about concerns that certain feelings are emerging within the context of the relationship—fantasies of Ellen taking care of him and images of himself in the role of "wife." Worries that his passivity and dependency will become a problem in the relationship. Patient also just found out that a termite poison, chlordane, is present in high levels in his building, although not above EPA standards for MA. Patient talked about his anxieties about his health and also about financial security—i.e. his apartment is all he owns, and he doesn't want its value to plummet.

July 21, 1988
Melinda R. Maron

Talked again about the chlordane situation and then about his worries that his hair might be falling out. Also talked about twitching before falling asleep, which Dr. Durendal had assured him not to worry about, and about some feelings of anxiety in his stomach that remind him of past depressions in which the tense, knotted feeling in his stomach was so intense that it was nearly unbearable. Patient says twitching at bedtime is also associated with subliminal fantasies of feeling threatened and vulnerable or feeling that he is about to do something he'll be punished for. Feels these tics etc. are less when he sleeps with Ellen and thought this had to do with release of sexual energies being relaxing.

August 4, 1988
Melinda R. Maron

Mr. S talked about his interest in primal therapy and his sense that only if he can discover and express some buried internal desires will he be able to move on in his life. Talked about his wish for this revelatory experience as similar to his religious experience in Opus Dei and something he might be able to repeat in therapeutic experience. Patient mentioned taboo in Opus Dei against making special friends and rule that everyone had to be treated equally. In some respects this was a relief to him, because he didn't have to worry about his lack of likable qualities.

August 11, 1988
Melinda R. Maron

Mr. S talked at length about his relationship and his anxiety that his girlfriend would idealize him and then become disillusioned and resentful. Patient worries whether he should be having more idealizing fantasies about her. Patient also talked about how he compares girl-friend and therapist.

August 18, 1988
Melinda R. Maron

Patient arrived feeling disconcerted about time. Says he's pressured about finishing an article and had wanted to reschedule apt. Talked about his irritation that relationship with his girlfriend takes so much time. He knows this is irrational. Transference issues of what he wants from therapist also discussed. Mr. S worried about developing feelings toward therapist.

August 28, 1988
Melinda R. Maron

Mr. S reported having a nightmare in which someone was in his apartment and he was in danger. He has this nightmare periodically. Talked about how uncomfortable fantasies of losing control are for him and arouse fear of being humiliated. He wondered whether feelings of anger and irritation with his girlfriend means he doesn't really care for her. Feels he would fall into "little fragments," however, if she were to get angry with him.

September 1, 1988
Melinda R. Maron

Reports having a memorable experience over the weekend. He was arguing about happiness with his girlfriend and suddenly felt very close. Patient still worries, however, about genuineness of his feelings.

Issues around transference also discussed—patient continues to compare therapist and girlfriend.

September 8, 1988
Melinda R. Maron

Reports feeling "down" at this time of year, when all the students come back and many of his friends move on to their teaching jobs, while he continues to feel like a failure without a career. Feels that if he lost his receptionist job, he'd be in trouble because he'd have to get a "real" job and wouldn't have time to be a freelance book reviewer. Somewhat reluctant to talk about how stuck and paralyzed he feels, worried the therapist will give up on him.

September 9, 1988
Deborah Lindwurm, MD
McLean Hospital

Initial meeting focused on Patient's report of his past depressions as well as his difficulties with obsessive thinking, indecisiveness, and "scrupulosity attacks." Feels he has been paralyzed emotionally and intellectually ever since he broke with his Catholic faith and left Opus Dei to study intellectual history. Currently on Parnate 50 mgs. The MAO diet and symptoms of hypertensive crisis were reviewed, and patient has a supply of nifedipine to use in this eventuality. He reports feeling somewhat low at this time of year. He is faced with his underachievement compared with friends who are college professors. He notes external stressors e.g. a deadline for a writing and a dispute over termiticide in his condo building. However, he denies loss of sleep, appetite, libido, or concentration. He is in a significant relationship with a female, Ellen.

September 15, 1988
Melinda R. Maron

Mr. S wanted to talk about relationship with Ellen and his discomfort with her being the more sexually assertive one in the relationship. Very concerned about hurting her feelings.

September 22, 1988
Melinda R. Maron

He was feeling upset because of an incident with a belligerent adolescent who threatened him. Led to a discussion of Mr. S's feelings about his own aggression and feelings of powerlessness and his envy of the adolescent's bravado. Theme of Mr. S's own aggression to explore.

September 29, 1988
Melinda R. Maron

No further upset about the adolescent but returned to discussion of his career and an interaction with an editor in which he felt devalued and very angry. Talked about how his anger felt too extreme for the circumstances. Wary of anger and the feelings of humiliation that often lie behind it.

October 6, 1988
Melinda R. Maron

Patient in a very self-deprecating mood, warning therapist about his complaining and capacity for distraction. Focus of session was on his tendency to "confess" what he feels are the "worst" aspects of himself in order to preempt others' disappointment or disapproval.

October 13, 1988
Melinda R. Maron

Talked at length about his anxiety re a presentation he will be making. He hasn't done this before and is afraid he will embarrass himself. Talking again about his feelings of failure but acknowledged he has had some successes this year. Mr. S. had a new haircut, which also seemed to be a source of some anxiety.

October 27, 1988
Melinda R. Maron

He talked about his envy of friends' successes and his guilt around feeling competitive and envious. Wonders if these feelings have caused him to lose early friendships. More talk of anxiety about upcoming presentation at B.U. English Department.

November 10, 1988
Melinda R. Maron

Mr. S talked again about getting inappropriately and disproportionately angry with people like mailmen, motorists, customer service representatives. Disappointed with himself for getting angry like this soon after a therapy session. His anger scares him because it seems to threaten the continuity of his relationship. Patient agreed he should learn to modulate anger.

November 17, 1988
Melinda R. Maron

Applying for a better job at Harvard. Reports feeling less phobic with some improved self-esteem due to therapy and his relationship.

December 1, 1988
Melinda R. Maron

Spent much of session talking about dependency, autonomy, and control. Patient feels his record buying is "out of control." Talked about his relationship with Ellen: he wishes she were more intelligent than he is but is uncomfortable when he suspects she is. Having difficulty reconciling his wish for the "ideal" woman with the reality of his present relationship.

December 20, 1988
Deborah Lindwurm, MD

Mr. Scialabba reports good mood, normal energy, appetite, and sleep. His relationship with his girlfriend is going well and he is doing quite a bit of freelance writing. He remains on Parnate 50 mg and c/o occasional tremors and myoclonic jerks.

December 22, 1988
Melinda R. Maron

Again discussed what he considered to be his "compulsive" record buying. Also mentioned that he became angry with his girlfriend, and then became very distressed when he saw the effect of his anger on her.

January 5, 1989
Melinda R. Maron

Patient went to NYC with girlfriend and reported having a very successful trip. Patient feeling better about the relationship, and his self-esteem, too, was more positive this week. He's also feeling better about his professional contacts and accomplishments.

January 5, 1989
Melinda R. Maron

This session involved discussion of Mr. S's body image and sexual themes. Underlying issues of perfectionism and disillusionment and how those issues affect his intimate relationships.

January 19, 1989
Melinda R. Maron

Patient wondering about going off medication. Talked about how paralyzed he'd been in the past by anxiety and depression. He is now able to tolerate small mishaps better, though he still feels unable to move ahead professionally.

January 26, 1989
Melinda R. Maron

Patient discussed his wish to resign as book review editor of *Zeta* magazine. He feels unappreciated by the other editors He feels guilty about quitting, even though he hasn't been paid for months. If he does quit, he'll be left only with his clerical job and his self-esteem will suffer. The decision is creating moderate anxiety.

February 2, 1989
Melinda R. Maron

Mr. Scialabba feeling quite depressed this week after seeing a friend's book on sale in the Harvard Book Store. Reminds him of "how little he's accomplished by comparison." He worries how friends and especially his girlfriend, think of him and his accomplishments, though he has been able to write more this year and was a finalist for an award for his book reviews. Patient feeling very guilty about not being able to feel more magnanimous toward his friend.

February 3, 1989
Deborah Lindwurm, MD

Mr. Scialabba reports continuing good spirits, with productivity as a writer, normal sleep, appetite, libido, and energy. His romantic relationship is very gratifying, and although he continues to feel that he is underachieving professionally, he has been pleased with his writing recently. He came in today requesting a trial off medication to ascertain whether Parnate is still needed.

February 9, 1989
Melinda R. Maron

Patient once again deciding whether to quit editing book review section of magazine. Finds himself again in conflict with editors but guilty about quitting and worried about the effect on his mood and self-esteem. Worried he won't be able to motivate himself to write with the extra time, though he has in the past.

February 16, 1989
Melinda R. Maron

Mr. S feeling anxious this week. Girlfriend has bought a house and he lent her money for it and offered support for her decision. Now anxious about the ways this may change their lifestyle together. Patient wishes security and being settled weren't so important and very critical of himself about it. Conflict evident between security, dependency, responsibility and freedom from responsibility and emotional ties.

February 23, 1989
Melinda R. Maron

Patient now feeling depressed about girlfriend's move. Anxious that it was the wrong decision and that the relationship won't survive it. But he saw it in context of other worries in the past that have kept him paralyzed. We will continue with the above.

March 2, 1989
Melinda R. Maron

Patient feeling much better about the move. Says he's adjusted much more readily than he expected. Patient then focused on career issues and his difficulty pursuing work that involves conflict. Talked about his style of avoiding conflict.

March 16, 1989
Melinda R. Maron

Patient received an award for his writing, which came with a cash award. Only partly able to enjoy this success; also kept devaluing and minimizing it. We talked about this conflict.

March 23, 1989
Melinda R. Maron

Patient trying to understand more about why he lacks commitment to writing and continues to procrastinate. Says he doesn't feel "worthy" or "deserving" to be a writer explored. Feels he's a "fake" and people will find out.

April 7, 1989
Deborah Lindwurm, MD

Patient has been taking Parnate 30 mg/d with fewer symptoms (lightheadedness) but similar efficacy. In spite of a recent flu-like illness his mood is stable and he denies vegetative symptoms. However, he is entering a time of year in which historically he is vulnerable to depression. He is reluctant to make any further change in his meds.

Pt. reminded of change in psychopharmacologists 7/1/89.

April 13, 1989
Melinda R. Maron

He reported that he'd been very ill with the flu and had to go to the infirmary for a couple of days with dehydration. Talked about his sense that his girlfriend was impatient with him. He worries about the relationship deteriorating into what his parents had. Also discussed what it was like to have someone angry with him.

April 20, 1989
Melinda R. Maron

He is still conflicted about quitting his book review editing job. Feels he must find a "moral" reason to leave rather than mere "gratification." Emerged that patient worries he'll be overwhelmed by strong affect and impulses if he allows himself to experience them even a little.

April 25, 1989
Melinda R. Maron

Talked about his ongoing difficulty with career decisions. Worries that his inability to act will frustrate therapist. Talked about how his relationship with Ellen has helped him to feel better about himself and more confident about his future, though his career still feels "stuck."

May 12, 1989
Melinda R. Maron

Patient talked about transference issues with therapist. Acknowledged that he flirts with women by ironically criticizing himself and making himself seem vulnerable. Talked about flirtation as a way of feeling in control and keeping distance from women.

May 19, 1989
Melinda R. Maron

Mr. Scialabba reported feeling unprepared for session and thus felt like he was "treading water." He was rejected for a teaching job he'd applied for at Harvard. Self-esteem was low. Talked about his ambivalence about teaching in general and whether or not that affected how he went about pursuing this job.

May 26, 1989
Deborah Lindwurm, MD

Patient reports continuing good spirits. Denies depressive symptoms. Is happy in his love relationship and looking forward to a trip to Oregon in June.

Plan: Continue Parnate 30 mg/d.

Patient to be transferred as of 6/30/89, will call me for name of new MD.

June 1, 1989
Melinda R. Maron

Focus of session again on career. He continues as book review editor and feels overwhelmed by its demands. Talked again about how difficult it is for him to say "no." Also acknowledged it was difficult to leave this job because of the money. Patient has planned a vacation with girlfriend.

June 8, 1989
Melinda R. Maron

Patient focused again on how difficult it is for him to deal with his critical feeling toward his girlfriend, Ellen. Finds it especially difficult to deal with her vulnerability and depressed or stressed moods. Admitted that part of the problem is that "he is the vulnerable one" and needs her to be strong and stable. Patient also talked about his difficulty with variations in sexual attraction. Talked about how intimacy involves times of not being able to idealize lovers and his fear of someone becoming dependent on him.

June 15, 1989
Melinda R. Maron

Last session before patient's vacation. He chose to focus on feelings of competitiveness and envy in relationship with a very successful friend, and how his guilt and self-consciousness about such feelings preventing him from engaging fully in the friendship.

June 26, 1989
Deborah Lindwurm, MD

Summary

The patient is a 40-year-old single white male who is a clerical worker at Harvard University. He is seen in weekly psychotherapy by Melinda Maron, LICSW.

The patient was initially seen in assessment by Dr. Juan Durendal on 7/23/87. He presented complaining of a past history of recurrent depression, as well as difficulties with obsessive thinking, indecisiveness and "scrupulosity attacks." He felt that he had been paralyzed intellectually and emotionally since he broke with his Catholic faith and left OPUS Dei to study intellectual history several years ago.

The patient was seen for over a year by Dr. Juan Durendal for psychopharmacology treatment. He was treated with Parnate, 50 mg daily which he tolerated fairly well apart from some orthostatic hypertension. He had no difficulty following the MAOI diet and had no symptoms suggestive of hypertensive crisis. He noted that the Parnate markedly alleviated his symptoms of depression, and both he and Melinda Maron felt that the Parnate helped with some of his obsessive ruminations. The case was transferred to me in 9/88 for continuation of MAOI therapy.

During the year I have seen Mr. Scialabba, he has not had any signs of symptoms of a major depressive episode. He has, however, complained of indecisiveness, procrastination, over-conscientiousness, and perfectionism, as well as feeling stalled in his life and "stuck" emotionally. He has struggled with feelings that he is underachieving from a professional point of view. From a psychopharmacology point of view, he was continued on Parnate at 50 mg/ per day until February 1989. At that point, Mr. Scialabba began reporting that he had felt quite good for some time and was experiencing more productivity as a writer. He was in the midst of a very gratifying romantic relationship, and requested a trial off medication to ascertain whether or not the Parnate was still needed. We discussed this and agreed to decrease

Parnate to 30 mg/ a day. Mr. Scialabba reports fewer side affects but similar efficacy from this lower dose. He was reluctant to further decrease the dose of medication because he was approaching the end of the academic year, which tended to be a vulnerable time for him in terms of depression. When he was last seen, in May of 1989, he was reporting continuing good spirits without vegetative signs of depression and with very few side effects of Parnate. He was having no difficulty at all adhering to the MAOI diet. At some point within the next year, he may request a trial off medication to see whether it is still necessary to manage his depressive symptoms.

July 6, 1989
Melinda R. Maron

Patient returned from vacation and reported that it had gone very well. He was surprised that he was able to forget about his problems long enough to enjoy himself. Was also relieved to be able to tolerate the intimacy issues of traveling with his girlfriend. Discussed patient's improved capacity to tolerate differences and disappointments in the relationship.

July 11, 1989
Amlie F. Eastman, MD
McLean Hospital

Pt. on stable dose of Parnate 30 mg qd. He reports rare lightheadedness episodes (fewer than when he took 50 mgqd). He reports his mood is stable and he denies vegetative symptoms of depression. We discussed the option of trying to change the med as was tried earlier this year. After careful discussion of his life stresses we agreed to make no changes at this time.

July 13, 1989
Melinda R. Maron

Patient again discussed his career doldrums. Talked a little abstractly about active/passive conflict as well as autonomy and dependency. Applied this to his relationship, where he worries about becoming dependent.

July 20, 1989
Melinda R. Maron

His mood somewhat more depressed, feeling dissatisfied with himself and his accomplishments and also feeling concerned about his girlfriend. He is anxious about the stress his girlfriend is under and her apparent symptoms of stress, such as a skin rash. Talked about his wishes for her to be the "strong" one, since he views himself as fragile and vulnerable. Worries that things will never change, that his girlfriend will always be stressed, and they will never share again the bliss of the early relationship. Patient talked about this as his "immaturity."

July 27, 1989
Melinda R. Maron

Patient very disturbed about his propensity to be late and about his obsessional behavior and rituals. Talked about what these behaviors meant in his life and what they were responses to. Also discussed some transference issues, such as patient's tendency to avoid talking about feelings regarding the therapist by intellectualizing. Talked about his fears of affects.

August 10, 1989
Melinda R. Maron

Patient continued discussing intimacy conflicts and work conflicts. Focused on feelings of humiliation and how his dependency stirs that particular affect. Related to relationship with mother and toilet behavior with her, which he felt very humiliated about.

August 17, 1989
Melinda R. Maron

Patient very distraught over misunderstanding with girlfriend. Feels confused about whether he really loves his girlfriend or just wants her to take care of him in ways he feels he can't take care of himself. Created moral dilemma for himself. If he suddenly got 3 million dollars, would he gladly share it with her? Or would he be relieved if she died? Patient very preoccupied with this.

September 8, 1989
Amelie F. Eastman, MD

Patient states in his late summer/early fall "funk" (i.e. depressed mood, "slow to bounce back," ruminations). He says this happens to him, every year and wondered if it were "back to school" time and he felt he hadn't gotten anywhere professionally. He reports that winter time is his "good time." He finds he has more energy, is happier, in general; described feeling "cheered-up" by the womb-like existence of winter time.

Patient denies any problems with med regimen. MSE was significantly different from law meeting with patient appearing worn-down with hunched posture. Speech was slow and deliberate, volume rather low (this seems baseline). Mood-depressed; affect—mildly depressed. No abnormal thought process or content. No SI/HI [suicidal ideation/homicidal ideation].

September 21, 1989
Melinda R. Maron

Patient managing better this fall. Depression has not become overwhelming. Attribute this to being in therapy and to being in a successful intimate relationship.

September 28, 1989
Melinda R. Maron

Patient planning to quit part-time job as book review editor. Very agitated about this; explored his anger and capacity to manage and express anger. Patient feels his capacity to function while angry has improved.

October 5, 1989
Melinda R. Maron

Patient continuing to focus on relationship: difficulties with intimacy and fears around dependency and autonomy. Discussed patient's reluctance to leave Harvard and feelings of competitive rivalry with friends, which leaves him feeling inadequate.

October 9, 1989
Melinda R. Maron

Patient beginning to focus more on transference issues, particularly dependency. He feels he's making progress: not as frightened of his own feelings and beginning to be able to connect them more immediately with experience.

October 13, 1989
Melinda R. Maron

Patient reports he was experiencing postural hypotension on 40 mg of Parnate. He lowered his own dose back to 30 mg. He says he did this partly because of the side effects and partly because he was through his "bad time of year." He noted that he "bounced back" well from a rejection of one of his articles earlier this week. His relationship with girlfriend remains strong. Sleep pattern has returned to normal. Continues to struggle with career direction and professional identity.

October 19, 1989
Melinda R. Maron

Patient continued to talk about imagined rivalry with friends. Also described relationship with mother, in which he felt the only way he could be separate was to succeed intellectually at school where he never had to compete to be the best. Was v. proud once when he and his brother beat up neighborhood bully. Patient unfamiliar with healthy competition and very guilty about his competitive wishes.

October 26, 1989
Melinda R. Maron

Patient feeling very disappointed about rejection of review he wrote. Discussed his feelings of vulnerability around any professional rejection. But feels he handled it better than he used to because he isn't so dependent on his professional self-esteem.

Patient also discussed his conflicts around commitment and his perfectionism and how he projects them onto girlfriend. Worried about declining sexual interest.

October 31, 1989
Melinda R. Maron

Problem No. 1:

Low self-esteem, hopelessness + underachievement resulting in depressed moods.

Goal (long term):

Stabilize mood and self-esteem.

Objectives (short term):

1. Help patient manage feelings of helplessness and dependency.
2. Modulate conflicts @ autonomy.
3. Help patient maintain intimate relationship.

Expected Achievement Date:

6/90

Specific Plans/Programs/Services:

Individual psychotherapy
Psychopharm

Frequency of Contact:

1x per week

Problem No. 2:

Obsessive compulsive symptoms which protect around anxiety, fears and affects in maladaptive way.

Goal (long term):

Decrease obsessive compulsive symptoms.

<u>Objectives (short term):</u>

   1. Patient will understand more about his anxieties and fears.

   2. Patient will begin to find new modes of managing anxiety.

<u>Termination Criteria:</u>

   Stabilized mood and self-esteem modified.

November 2, 1989
Melinda R. Maron

   Patient in good mood because his review has been accepted at *Nation*. Talked again about his dependency on girlfriend; specifically, his fear of being dependent on her rather than being in love with her. Began to touch on issue of hostile dependency.

November 8, 1989
Melinda R. Maron

   Patient concerned about being out of touch with his feelings. Still wants therapist to tell him what is getting in the way of feeling. Wonders if he'll ever change.

December 14, 1989
Melinda R. Maron

   Focus on patient's compulsive behaviors, cleaning, storing clothing, organizing + re-organizing. Talked about anxiety and how it contributes to procrastination. Other aspects of compulsive behavior noted.

December 28, 1989
Melinda R. Maron

~~Met with Mr. Scialabba for 50 minutes.~~ (Error). No meeting with Mr. Scialabba this week. Therapist away.

January 4, 1990
Melinda R. Maron

He reported feeling somewhat depressed around the New Year: still feeling stuck in life. Feels he would be even more depressed if he weren't in a relationship. As before, envy of friends leads to feelings of low self-esteem.

January 25, 1990
Melinda R. Maron

Focused on his wish that he would be cured by understanding why he left Opus Dei. Discussed why he sees his decision to leave the Church as the cause of all his difficulties.

February 1, 1990
Melinda R. Maron

Very anxious about girlfriend's stress and worries about developing resentment toward her. Feels they can't both be depressed at the same time. He expressed frustration, anger, resentment, confusion.

March 1, 1990
Melinda R. Maron

He's read an article about narcissism and decided that many of his difficulties began in his early relationship with his mother.

March 6, 1990
Amelie F. Eastman, MD

Mood "not bad." Life fairly busy recently. Still with girlfriend—things going well. Diminished sex drive over the past 6 months, but otherwise no symptoms of depression. Meds now Parnate 30 mg qd.

March 8, 1990
Melinda R. Maron

He's exploring his career options. Feeling very dependent on girlfriend/fiancée for future economic support. Worried that he has little to offer in return.

March 22, 1990
Melinda R. Maron

Talked about compulsive behaviors and how difficult they are to change. His compulsions are limiting but not out of control. They're somewhat dystonic, but mostly he wants reassurance about them. We discussed how compulsions contribute to procrastination. He's developing some insight about this.

March 31, 1990
Melinda R. Maron

Problem No. 1:

Low self-esteem, hopelessness and underachievement resulting in depressed moods and difficulties in intimate relationship.

Goal (long term):

Stabilize mood and self-esteem.

Objectives (short term):

1) Help patient to modulate conflicts @ ___ .
2) Patient will have stable intimate relationships.
3) Patient will be less critical of himself and his achievements.

Problem No. 2:

Obsessive compulsive symptoms which protect against anxiety, fears, affects in maladaptive style.

Objectives (short term):

1. Patient will continue to gain insight re: anxiety and fears.
2. Patient will find ways of dealing with anger.
3. Patient will develop more understanding of way obsessive compulsive symptoms interfere with his functioning.

Termination Criteria:

Stabilized moods and self-esteem + modified obsession compulsive symptoms.

May 10, 1990
Melinda R. Maron

Talked about what was interfering with making a commitment (permanent) to his girlfriend and examined his difficulty continuing to feel sexual desire. Very guilty about his sexual fantasies which make him question himself and relationship. Actually seems more tolerant of his impulses and aware that he's not going to act on them.

September 6, 1990
Melinda R. Maron

He described a fairly successful month at writer's colony, although he found himself avoiding internal conflicts and powerful affects. Felt very positive about relationship with girlfriend. Seemed very good for self-esteem.

September 13, 1990
Melinda R. Maron

He reports having some difficulty making the transition back to work. Finds himself for some reason obsessively preoccupied with clothes and also with housecleaning. Also, realizing how much money his girlfriend makes was a blow to his self-esteem and left him feeling less secure in the relationship.

December 18, 1990
Dr. Brannigan
McLean Hospital

Termination Note
  Scialabba, George
  MR#042941

The patient suffers in a typical depression which has been well stabilized on Parnate 30 mg poqd. The patient suffers minimal side effects of orthostatic hypotension which has not interfered with his functioning at work or at home. Because of financial constraints the patient would like to close his chart at the AOPC with follow up by Dr. Cindy Shepard, at the Harvard Health Services Clinic. The patient requested to be able to return to the AOPC if he needs a re-assessment should there be a change in his psychiatric condition.

I discussed the situation with Mr. Scialabba in person and on the telephone on Dec. 17 and reiterated that he is welcomed to return to the AOPC for re-assessment at any time.

March 7, 1991
Melinda R. Maron

Final Summary

Date of Initiation of Treatment:
  7/87

Frequency and Length of Sessions:
  Mr. Scialabba met on a 1 time weekly basis for 50 minute session between 7/87 and 2/91. He came consistently to, missing only for illness and vacations.

Brief Summary of Identifying Data/Presenting Problem:

Mr. Scialabba is a 42-year-old white, single male who works full-time in a clerical position at Harvard University. He is also a writer of book reviews and essays for literary journals. Initial presenting problem: felt depressed and "stalled" in his life and wanted medication. It was recommended that he try a MAOI and enter long-term exploratory therapy with a female therapist. During the initial diagnostic phase of therapy, it was determined that patient had difficulty expressing and modulating affects, managing conflicts around aggression and sexuality, and achieving relatedness and intimacy with other people. He was extremely perfectionistic and hard on himself. These were the dynamic issues to be pursued in therapy.

Summary of Treatment:

During the course of treatment, which included psychopharmacology and psychotherapy, Mr. Scialabba's depression markedly improved and his rigidity, obsessional compulsions, and inhibitions also modulated and became less dysfunctional for him.

Initially Mr. Scialabba believed very strongly, that his problems stemmed from his leaving a strict lay religious order, Opus Dei, and that if he could relive what had happened to him then, there would be an emotional catharsis and he would be "cured." Although he still holds this belief, he has worked very hard at explaining other aspects of his life and personality. He has become a successful writer, although he minimizes this and continues to see himself as professionally paralyzed. He is right in that he continues to be unable to leave Harvard or to commit himself to something more ambitious, but he has improved. Mr. Scialabba has also been able to maintain a serious intimate relationship with a woman, and his current relationship appears to be a mature, healthy one. His conflicts around dependency and autonomy, as well as his perfectionistic and narcissistic issues, continue to be areas of struggle and anguish for him, but he has been able to stay in the relationship.

Transference phenomena have included an idealized, at times

sexualized, transference, with patient feeling like a much less powerful person, even like a child, and hoping for an omnipotent object
to solve his pain. Patient has formed a positive, working alliance with
the therapist and has shown a remarkable capacity to engage in in-
depth psychotherapy. It is only because of his financial situation that
he cannot be seen twice a week. Patient will continue in long-term psychotherapy with Dr. Maron on a private basis. He decided to terminate
from the AOPC because he could not afford the clinic fee.

Final Diagnosis and Assessment:

Mr. Scialabba terminated from the clinic with this depression
in remission. He continues on an MAOI prescribed and monitored
through Harvard University Health Services. His obsessional ruminations and behaviors have also improved. He continued to experience
internal conflicts and inhibitions around expression of affects, dependency, and work, although the intensity of these were mitigated by
some successful experiences in his relationships and with his writing.

The Knot of Anxiety (1991–1994)

December 6, 1991
Allan Woodcourt, MD
Harvard University Mental Health Services

Mr. Scialabba is a 43-year old, single building manager at Harvard
who had a significant history of depression. Some of his autobiograph-
ical information is in a 3-page write-up that he brought with him. His
depression came on shortly after he left a Roman Catholic order. He
saw Dr. Franklin here at UHS who started him on desipramine, to
which he responded very quickly. Then in about 1987, he again became
severely depressed and was seen at the McLean Hospital Outpatient
Department where he was begun on Parnate and started in psychotherapy with Ms. Melinda Maron. He's continued the psychotherapy
since and has also continued the Parnate with doses ranging from 30

to 50 mg a day. He feels that the Parnate has helped him to be less obsessive and has helped his depression somewhat, but he still feels very much stuck in his life with a kind of low-grade depressed feeling which lingers.

Although he's continued in his therapy, he's not had any psycho-pharmacological follow-up since about 1989, as his medications have been provided by Dr. Shepard. He scheduled the appointment today specifically to talk over medication questions. Apparently the possibility of putting him on Prozac has never come up. My thought is that for the kind of chronic low-grade obsessive-depressive picture that he presents, Prozac might be the drug of choice, though it really wasn't perhaps available when he first started Parnate back in 1987. He seemed to feel that this would be worth a try and so, after discussing various questions at length about his theories about depression and about the psychotherapeutic theories of Arthur Janov in which he's quite interested, we decided that he would taper the Parnate by 10 mg a day every 4 days until he's off. That will take 16 days and that he would then remain off the drug for 14 days, following which time we could start fluoxetine. He scheduled a follow-up appointment for January 3.

December 26, 1991
Allan Woodcourt, MD

He called to say that he has now been off Parnate for 3 days and is not feeling well. He is depressed, he is agitated, his appetite is down and he's having trouble sleeping. He's particularly worried in that his bad mood he feels is making him cruel to his girlfriend, although she apparently is being very good about it. I told him that we would really have to wait 2 weeks before he could start the Prozac, but that I would be willing to try to tide him over with Oxazepam, 15 mg up to 4 po qd, #40, no refills to help him with some of these symptoms in the meantime. He also tells me that his mother tried Prozac a year or so ago and gave it up because it caused her so much agitation and tremulousness.

I told him I didn't think that would necessarily happen in his case and in any case we could start dosing at lower rates and go up more slowly. He was also concerned about the interval of time that it would take for the Prozac to work and whether or not the improvement that he got with Prozac would really be any better than what he had with the Parnate and in short, there's clearly some anxiety and hesitancy but he's willing to continue with the plan and so we will meet again on January 3, 1992.

February 13, 1992
Allan Woodcourt, MD

Yesterday Mr. Scialabba was admitted to the Stillman Infirmary because his feelings of agitation and depression had simply become unbearable. He had called me the day before and I had left a prescription for Ativan but he had not picked that up. Once in the infirmary, Dr. Motek started him on propranolol, 20 mg big and lorazepam, 0.5 mg bid as a way of managing what was possibly an akathetic component to the increased fluoxetine dose. He felt better immediately upon admission and I saw him today, at which point it came out that his feelings of agitation and desperateness were quite similar to his prior depressions, and that they did not seem to increase in a manner too terribly correlated with the dose of Prozac, and though his hives had continued at a low level, he had had hives as a child, and that in his earlier depressions there had been a sense of flushing of the skin. He was very concerned about some upcoming dental work and also about whether he would be able to handle all the logistic problems which he needs to get out of town on Mar. 24 and meet his girlfriend at a house in France and then travel with her for two weeks. Meanwhile she is away in the Pacific Northwest and then will go to France to stay in a rented house and wait for him to come. Thus, he's feeling very much alone and that all kinds of demands are put upon him which he's not confident that he can fulfill.

It's very confusing to know what to do in terms of medications. I did talk with his therapist, Dr. Melinda Maron, and she's continuing to meet with him. On the one hand since the urticaria is continuing, it probably is reasonable to discontinue the Prozac and not wait further for a response possibly to the increased dose. Also there is some possibility that he is experiencing akathesia which would be possibly manageable with propranolol, although that's not clear. If we are to put him back on the Parnate, we would have to wait 5 weeks after discontinuing the fluoxetine, and that would just about get him to the time of his departure in late March. But that leaves the situation fairly unclear both up to then and after he leaves. He does remember a tricyclic having been used during his first episode of depression and he does feel that that was probably effective. Also, it turns out his mother had been on Prozac at a low dose and had felt very jittery on it, though he describes her as someone with a very low threshold for discomfort. What I decided to do is to start him on nortriptyline 25 mg, and to discontinue the Prozac for now and see if the urticaria disappears. If it does not, we can presume that it is not Prozac-related, I might resume Prozac at 10 mg in the morning and have him on both medications. If it does go away then we might try managing the depression with a tricyclic drug. Then, after he returns from his two-week trip, we can assess the situation again and decide whether to resume the Parnate or not. I will continue to follow him in Stillman until he's discharged.

February 25, 1992
Allan Woodcourt, MD

He said his moods go up and down during the week, although in the past few days he has felt, as he puts it, 7 ½ on a scale of 10, with 0 being the state he was in in the Infirmary and 10 being his normal state. He is having some dry mouth, some constipation, and some mental slowing, although it's better than the agitation he was experiencing. He re-challenged himself by taking 10 mg of Prozac mornings and thought he felt flushed, though he's not sure if it was hives or not. I told him that if he wanted to experiment by taking 10 mg of Prozac again for several days, that would not be dangerous, it would be completely up to him. He has many concerns about the medications. He has been reading lots and lots of self-help books and in particular a book called *Toxic Psychiatry* by Peter Breggin, and as a result is showing signs of feeling really quite uncomfortable with the whole idea of medications, for which one cannot blame him given what he's been through. However, today he will get a nortriptyline level and remain on nortriptyline 75 mg until I see him again on March 3. He continues to meet with his therapist, Dr. Melinda Maron.

June 26, 1992
Allan Woodcourt, MD

He is not doing well at all. He has been on Parnate at a dose of about 50 mg a day for approximately five weeks and he still feels depressed all the time, with extreme difficulty concentrating and getting any work done, with fragmented sleep and reduced appetite, and complete loss of libido. One of the precipitants is the fact that his girlfriend has now gone to Africa, and this in the context of her feeling more and more anxious about the burden that he might be and about whether or not his depression would ever get better. He is frustrated with his therapy with Melinda Maron because it hasn't done more for him, and he comes in today looking limp and with sighing respirations. A somewhat low and slowed voice, though his mind is still active and he still has many questions to ask me. As he relates the story now, all of this began after he left Opus Dei and he feels it is related to some enormous guilt stemming from that. As he describes it now, he had a period of intense agitated anxiety that lasted for months and months after he left the order, and which, in a sense, has never quite gone away.

July 13, 1992
Allan Woodcourt, MD

He tells me that his moods have not been as good in the past week as they were when I last saw him. Prior to that he had had an experience of recovering the lost feelings from the days before he was in Opus Dei, but now he feels that those are somewhat more distant. Current issues that may be leading to the downturn is that his girlfriend is due to be back in a few days and he went to a party over the weekend which was discouraging in that other people there seemed to be doing so much better than he was career-wise. He brings me more books on psychopharmacology, with more questions about the Parnate and so on. We discussed various options, including getting an MAO level and adding lithium.

August 18, 1992
Allan Woodcourt, MD

He comes in looking rather badly. He is on verge of tears, feeling completely discouraged and depressed, unable to write and feeling hopeless about the relationship with Ellen and particularly about his own moods. He has not been on the lithium for a little over a month and on Parnate at 60 mg a day and it's hard to feel that that's a success, but yet he's also quite discouraged with me and reluctant to make any changes, since, as he says, he isn't as desperate and agitated as he was when he started the Parnate. We left it that he would get another lithium level (it was .39 on a dose of 900 mg), and that I would talk with his therapist, Melinda Maron, and also that he would call Dr. George Ellwood about the possibility of a private consultation to provide some advice as to where to go next with the medications. It's not that I lack any idea of what to do next, but he really is feeling discouraged with all the changes that he and I have been though and another perspective might be helpful, at least consultatively. He and I will meet again on August 27.

August 27, 1992
Allan Woodcourt, MD

Things seem a little calmer this week. He had a good weekend with Ellen, and does not seem so despairing, although he says yesterday morning he was quite tearful, and so it's not clear that there's any real improvement. What he complains of mostly now is a sort of knot of anxiety which he locates in his stomach and which he feels really inhibits him. He feels that a medication might be the best treatment for that, but although Buspar might be a good choice, that can't be done while he's on Parnate. We planned that we would temporize again for another couple of weeks and not make any changes. He has a lithium level due back soon. I gave him prescriptions for Lithobid 300 mg, m 2 po rid, #100 no refills and also tranylcypromine 10 mg, 3 po bid, #130 with no refills. He is considering whether or not he wishes to consult with Dr. Ellwood and hasn't made up his mind finally about that. He'll be back to me on September 11.

October 16, 1992
Allan Woodcourt, MD

He doesn't report much change over the week, but perhaps a little bit less anguish and despair, although there is some sense of lightheadedness which is not related to standing up from a chair. He is taking the Klonopin at a rate of about 1 mg a day, and this may be associated with some decrease in feelings of agitation, although he does report some lethargy, particularly later in the day. We talked a lot about strategies and at the moment he wants to perhaps think about reducing the dose of Parnate to 40 mg over the next week and seeing how things ago. He's also very interested in looking at all of his UHS records, apparently because of some dispute with his girlfriend about whether he was or was not in complete despair through the first three months of 1992. He also raises the issue as to whether the Parnate was tapered too quickly in December, 1991 and whether this may have had something to do with all that he has suffered since. On looking at that record, I see that he reduced his dose by 10 mg every 4 days, and that during the first 3 days he was off he did have some symptoms of agitation and decreased appetite and trouble sleeping, which I had suggested he cover with some oxazepam, which he did not in fact take because he improved by early January and by mid-January was not having any symptoms that could be in any way ascribed to withdrawal. I gave him another prescription for Parnate, 10 mg, to take 4 or 5 po a day, #100, no refills and I will see him again on October 23.

January 26, 1993
Allan Woodcourt, MD

He is feeling miserable: lethargic, depressed, tearful, unable to concentrate, sleeping eight hours a night but unable to get out of bed for an hour after he wakes up, and feeling quite bleak and hopeless about things. Part of it is that he has not heard favorable word about his book, and part of it is that Ellen seems to be drifting further away from him. As usual at times like this, he is thinking of changing therapists and not seeing Melinda Maron any more, though she called me today. He is not suicidal. As he sits in the office there is a great deal of sighing and groaning and slumping in the chair, but occasionally he does laugh. He has only been on the 50 mg of sertraline for about six or seven days and so it's too soon to decide that that is not working. He is taking it at night, and it's not certain whether that is helping his lethargy at all. He's still using the Klonopin, but only at the rate of about .5 mg a day. He pressures a great deal that something should be done and that he cannot stand things anymore, and I thought perhaps, pursuant to Dr. Ellwood's earlier suggestions, we might as well add the Buspar. I wrote him the following prescriptions: buspirone 5 mg one po tid, times three, then add one po qd, every three days, #36 with no refills and buspirone 10 mg one po tid, to start when the 5 mg ½ po qd. #30 with no refills and clonazepam 0.5 mg up to one po ti prn, #60 with no refills. He wants very much to come in next week instead of in two weeks and so we arranged a check-in visit on February. He asked me whether he should go to New York and see friends even though he was feeling so terrible, and I strongly encouraged him to do it, reminding him that other times when he had gone to see friends his mood had lifted a bit.

February 2, 1993
Allan Woodcourt, MD

He says that things are much worse, that he's feeling hopeless and that he's suffering intensely, but he does say that he went to New York and although he found it very tiring and a lot of work, he said it was "diverting" to see his friends. He looks extremely downcast today with a lot of slow talking and great deal of sighing respiration, and was wanting to know whether or not I thought it would be advisable for him to go to the hospital or to have ECT, neither of which I think is a good idea at this time. Though I didn't ask specifically about it, he did not mention anything that made me think that suicide was a risk, and also I did have a conversation with his therapist Ms. Melinda Maron last week, and she agrees that suicide is not a risk now but further regression certainly is. My sense is that he should remain out of the hospital at this point. Though he is depressed, he really does seem to be caring for himself adequately and he is going to work every day and seeing friends. He brought me in something from the Harvard Mental Health Letter which suggested that the dose of sertraline could be as high as 200 mg a day, and I also thought that since he's been on the sertraline for approximately three weeks with no benefit yet at 50 mg he might just as well increase to 100 mg. He has not had any side effects from the Buspar and is just about to begin that at a dose of 30 mg a day. He uses the Klonopin .5 mg only at night, because the .5 mg makes him too sleepy if he takes it during the day, and when I asked him whether he could split it in half and take a half of one, he said that splitting the pill was almost too much effort for him. Yet he's clearly able to read and does a lot of reading, though mostly on depression and psychopharmacology. He has not heard any word from his book agent, which I think is deeply discouraging. We arranged to meet again in one week, although he wished that there be someone at the UHS who could meet with him every day. I told him that that would not be possible to arrange on an appointment basis but did remind him of the availability of the Urgent Care Clinic. He has also heard good things about Dr. Berl from someone in Coolidge Hall and wonders if he might help him. I suggested that if he wished to consult with Dr. Berl he was certainly free to do that.

March 23, 1993
Allan Woodcourt, MD

He presents me today with a rating of his moods which he has devised. Things still do look kind of bleak according to the numbers, but as we talk about it in more detail, it appears there has been some improvement. He is still very anhedonic and feels very blocked in his writing. However, the desperation is a bit less. In terms of medications, I thought that perhaps a continued reduction in the sertraline, which hasn't proved to be much use, and after we reviewed together his whole record of his treatment with me we decided that perhaps the desipramine had been of some help after all, although there was constipation and dry mouth, and so he would prefer at this point to go back to that again rather than to try Wellbutrin or go back to Parnate. Thus, he will now reduce his sertraline to 50 mg po qam, reduce his busiprone to 20 mg po qd and add desipramine 25 mg, one po qhs. And then perhaps slowly increasing towards 3 po qhs, #21 with no refills and will be back to me on March 31.

July 13, 1993
Allan Woodcourt, MD

He's continued to improve and had a marvelous time at the Mc-Dowell Writer's Colony. According to his rating sheet, he's improved in all areas, with the least good showing being in his sex drive which has improved to a minus 2 from a minus 4. He discontinued busiprone several days ago and didn't notice anything from that, and has also decided to remain in a break from his therapy for now. He still feels that he's not as mentally flexible as he was before the episode of depression and that he has a harder time moving back and forth between present and past, although he finds himself more firmly rooted in the present now. He also talked about tension in his jaw and about how when he experiencing anything whether good or bad, he tends to express it in tension in the jaw muscles, and that for many years he's been a tooth grinder and has a mouth guard to wear at night. I talked about relaxation training as a possible way to approach that and will sign him up for it. I also wrote him for sertraline, 100 mg, ½ po qam, #30, no refills and will see him again on August 3.

November 5, 1993
Allan Woodcourt, MD

His mood continues good, but he continues to have difficulty achieving an erection. This is not only a loss to him, but it may be more of a problem in that he has now met someone new whom he likes a lot. They haven't been involved sexually yet, but he thinks that that may come. We talked about various ways of managing it, including adding cyproheptadine, reducing the dose of sertraline back to 50 mg since the 100 mg. Didn't seem to help much (yet he's had this symptom even on 50 mg), and switching to Wellbutrin, which he has never been on. My sense is that in some ways it's a shame to rock the boat, whereas it's not certain that the Zoloft actually produced the improvement he now enjoys, one hates to change something which at least appears to be working. H agreed with the idea of waiting another month to see where the relationship goes and to see whether in fact the sexual problem is a real problem or not. Then when we meet again we can consider perhaps a switch. He needs no medications today, we'll reduce his dose to 50 mg, and will be back on December 2.

December 30, 1993
Allan Woodcourt, MD

All in all, he's really doing quite well, although there have been moments when he has felt badly about himself and obsessed about the fact that he hadn't accomplished as much as he would have liked, by and large things have been upbeat and he is working. His relationship with Janice is continuing to go well, and this I think has a great deal to do with the improvement. He did reduce the dose of sertraline to 50 mg a day, and still finds it's very difficult to reach orgasm although he considers himself to be functioning well sexually and we decided to leave things alone. I wrote him for sertraline, 100 mg, ½ po qam, #15, no refills and will see him again on January 27.

April 14, 1994
Allan Woodcourt, MD

He's continued along on a more or less even keel, and the relationship with Janice has continued as well. His sexual function is perhaps a little better and he hasn't used the cyproheptadine at all practically speaking, and I told him if he ever did want to try it he could take it in the morning rather than having to wait until 2 hours prior to intercourse. He feels that his stability has been purchased at some cost in terms of affective range, but as we talked over the misery of the past year I think he is willing not to rock the boat for the moment. He's looking forward to his summer plans and is keeping on with his writing although he isn't achieving the kind of ambitious projects that he had at one time felt he needed to do. We will meet again June 2. I wrote him a prescription for sertraline, 100 mg ½ po qam, #30, no refills.

Pieces of Life (1996)

April 30, 1996
Allan Woodcourt, MD
Harvard University Mental Health Services

He remains feeling better than he did a few weeks ago, and says he doesn't have the agitated feeling he's had during his severe depressions, but his outlook is very gloomy and he views himself as someone who has been more or less completely disabled since he left the Opus Dei religious order in 1969. He has seen Janice a couple of times and doesn't now have the feeling that she's bored with him, but overall his outlook is much gloomier than it has been, and I think there is some significant depression. He doesn't disagree with this, but somehow he prefers to see the problem as related to a permanent disability rather than related to mood. He talked about going back into psychotherapy again, and I indicated that I would be very willing to help him arrange that on a sliding-scale basis that he could afford.

May 28, 1996
Bert Milliner, PhD, MPH
Harvard University Health Services, Psychiatric Clinic

Mr. Scialabba is 48, born in Boston and grew up in East Boston. His parents are living, married, and live in East Boston. He is the second of two, with an older brother. He is single, never married, in a relationship with Janice, 45 or 46, an editor and writing her dissertation. The relationship has been ongoing for 2½ years and Mr. Scialabba has no children. He does not have a lot of friends but has a few. He has a master's degree in History, is a building manager at the International Studies Center, but spends much time on freelance book reviews. He has been at the Center for 16 years. He lives in Cambridge alone, does not smoke, does not drink, does not use any drugs, has no history of these, no family history of use, and in terms of psychiatric history, he had a first cousin who committed suicide at 21. He notes his mother is a severely dysthymic and severely obsessional person, diagnoses which have been applied to him by an eminent psychiatrist and which seem to ring true to him. He has no physical problems and takes Zoloft, up to 250 mg at this time, although he was on a maintenance dose for three years of 50 mg. He does not get very regular exercise, jogs once a week and does 5–10 minutes of calisthenics each morning. In terms of psychological treatment, he has been in psychotherapy a number of times, he would say unsuccessfully, only once for more than a year. He has had two clinical depressions in the last 15 years, both for several months, but pretty awful. He has seen Dr. Woodcourt for about five years.

He presents today noting that he was a little shaken by the episode six weeks ago. He does not know what brought it on, noting he wound up psychodynamic therapy three years ago after five years. It was someone he liked but it didn't seem to help. He thinks his concerns are partly biochemical and he is grateful for Zoloft.

He came across a number of articles that say cognitive therapy has the highest success rate, so he read *Feeling Good* and one or two books by Aaron Beck, although he is rather scornful of these. He is sympathetic to psychoanalytic ideas, but he has been humbled by these depressions.

The overall problem he notes was that he was a very devout Catholic, part of a religious order, which he left at 21 during the summer between college and graduate school. He was so agitated he had to drop out of graduate school. Seemingly, the pieces of his life never came back together. He did not feel able to do any intellectual work, never resumed his life again. When he tried to read philosophy or political history, he was unable to focus, felt a certain background tension. For the past 15 years, he has been in literary criticism, written about 150 book reviews, won a national award. However, it is not the same as having a career and he still feels kind of disabled. On a micro-level, he has always been very obsessive, fretful, replaying decisions, defensive and feeling he has to defend himself against imagined threats although he has never been delusional or psychotic.

I explained our more focused and briefer time frame and noted if he was going to begin something that would be longer term, he'd want to actually change his basic affect. He never went back to graduate school because he didn't think he could handle it, and although he would not choose to do so now, he would want to feel he could. He seemingly had felt that if he pulled out all the stops, he would freeze up. If we had only a few sessions, he would want me to convince him to decide on whether to go on in terms of therapy and what kinds of therapy it would be or what realistic goals he might set.

I briefly explained my view of cognitive therapy as involving the belief system of both the therapist and the patient and involving the belief that one's cognitions could affect one's experience and one's feelings. He said this sounded reasonable to him and that he was ready to try anything. We set a follow-up for June 17, at 10:00 a.m.

June 17, 1996
Bert Milliner, PhD, MPH

Mr. Scialabba noted his having mentioned his inclination to defend himself against counter-attack but he now notes another issue too, which is envy. He just keeps comparing himself to other people's success, especially if it is someone he is competitive with, and he notes one person who started out at the same time as he did as a freelance literary critic and is now successful and has a family.

In terms of our discussion, he noted that when he is with his girlfriend, he often wonders if he has said or done something kind of immature, or when she is very tired and quiet, he thinks he is dull or has said something to upset her. He sees her 2–4 times a week and this occurs 2–3 times in each visit. If we were successful in working on this, this would occur less frequently. I gave him a weekly report form, asked him about recording when this occurs, which he would do afterwards.

He seemed to relate the idea of doing something wrong and being punished, noting that fear is the basis of his moral psychology. I explained the idea of logical analysis of his thoughts versus simple thought-stopping. Both appeal to him, but we focused on thought-stopping and concluded when he has the first thought of his being boring etc., he would immediately stop that thought and pursue a different pathway. He noted liking when she teaches him about things, they have good sex and good pillow talk, which might be alternative thoughts for him.

August 26, 1996
Bert Milliner, PhD, MPH

Mr. Scialabba said he was doing pretty well, noting that the defensive response and his self-doubting have both been pretty much under control. He also then noted a tendency to put his hands on his face, monitored that, and found that it really reduced the frequency of the behavior. He focused then on a more substantive issue: his coming late to work. His hours are from 11:00 a.m. to 5:00 but tends to come 30–45 minutes late. I initially focused on the source, with his noting some resentment about his position, which is not a professional position, but he does not really contemplate changing the job. I suggested we consider his anger/resentment, work that through a bit and thus permit him to deal with the job without coming late. The next strategy involved his selecting a reinforcer for himself, earned if he got to work less than 30 minutes late, or less than 15, and then on time. I also noted his ability to think of himself as doing what he says, coming to work on time because he said he would. He suggests that he is "lazy and sneaky." I challenged these self-descriptions, noted he could transform them. He noted in the past having masturbated regularly and did not feel he could control it. Seemed to feel this was tied in with his major depressions. We may discuss that further.

September 3, 1996
Bert Milliner, PhD, MPH

Mr. Scialabba reported that he had actually gotten to work on time, by 11:30 a.m., about four out of five days since our last appointment. He did not know why but felt that talking about it with an authority figure must have meant something. He then noted a trait of his, being unable to get right down to the important issue, for example, having to be sure his desk was neat and pencils sharpened before he could go to work. We did discuss his self-perception, noting his having a persistent sense of not being entirely grown up. He has the mental ability to have a professional career and the desire but he has not done this. When he left graduate school and the religious order, he anticipated going back to graduate school but his depression never cleared up sufficiently to allow that.

Asked if we had 6–8 sessions to try to focus on the resolution of this issue that his life has grown around, he was unsure of goals he might set. He seemed to feel that by staying on the surface, he avoids the depths of depression, whereas if he tried to set his life right from the ground up, he might go into a depression. I noted his options and he felt he might really want to go along as a better freelance writer, not wanting to do anything different but feeling differently about it. He spoke again about the feelings he had when in the Church, which were very intense and which he felt would be his emotional core but that disappeared behind a veil when he left.

September 12, 1996
Bert Milliner, PhD, MPH

Mr. Scialabba has shown some slippage in getting to work on time, but on the whole he's still doing better. We discussed the issue of his moving forward at this point in terms of the concept of the curtain that dropped on his emotional life, August 18, 1969, which was the day he left Opus Dei, the Catholic religious order he had been in through college. Although it was for laymen, they did take vows of poverty, chastity and obedience. He had to decide between law school (their preference) or grad school (his preference), wound up applying to and registering for both, in great turmoil, and felt this indecision was disgraceful and that he had to do something definitive. So he left Opus Dei. The following year was wracked by agitation. I explained my view that at 21 he was dealing with intellectual efforts to control his sexuality, that in the past 20 or 30 years he has changed and grown significantly, and that this would enable him to approach the problem in a different way now.

September 19, 1996
Bert Milliner, PhD, MPH

We returned to his conviction that he cannot go forward until he recovers the feelings that were covered over by the disturbance of his leaving the Church. I suggested those feelings were tied to his developmental stage at that time and therefore he could never really recapture them, and that it might be unnecessary to try. I suggested that he might have access to the energies presumably locked away by virtue of thinking about them with a different metaphor.

Worm's-Eye View (2000–2005)

June 5, 2000
Allan Woodcourt, MD
Harvard University Mental Health Services

He had an upwelling of thirty-year-old depression and panic as he was reviewing a book which dealt with Thomism and brought back his feelings upon leaving Opus Dei, which led to his first major depression.

He was astonished at how intense the feelings were after 30 years. But they subsided, and he's now at his baseline. At the same time, friends and acquaintances have had publishing and romantic success, which has also been a precipitant for him in the past. We talked about the advisability of going back into therapy for a while. He says he doesn't have the energy or money now but was somewhat interested in thinking about it if the number of insurance-covered sessions increased after January.

March 23, 2001
Allan Woodcourt, MD

He's been stable. His father is weakening, and he feels he won't live more than another two months. He may have to cancel his spring trip to Big Bend. He's met a woman, Catalina, who's a pediatric neurologist. They've been going out since January. He'll be back in three months.

October 17, 2002
Allan Woodcourt, MD

His physical symptoms have improved, and he's feeling well. He had a conversation with a colleague which brought him face to face with the fact that his current job will probably disappear in two years. For several days he was as agitated as he was when he left Opus Dei 20 years ago, and he feared a relapse. But the feelings settled down, and he was able to see that he's more resilient than he was then, and that there are various ways he could survive without that job. On the other hand, he'd like more support as he contemplates the transition, and we agreed to meet again in a month, on November 14.

Current medications: sertraline 200 mg qam

November 14, 2002
Allan Woodcourt, MD

He became very anxious when he called BU about teaching English composition. We talked more about the time, twenty years ago, when he left Opus Dei. He felt initially that he was wrong to stay when he had doubts, then that he was wrong to leave. Apparently they wanted him to go to law school, for their purposes, while he wanted to go to graduate school and become a college teacher of humanities.

Because this a particularly hard time, I suggested he increase his sertraline to 250 mg. He would also like a referral to a CBT [cognitive behavioral therapist], to help manage the anxiety.

July 17, 2003
Allan Woodcourt, MD

He came down with a virus and became extremely tired. Dr. Simmons found nothing medically wrong but suggested the fatigue might be a form of his depression. In the past two days he's plunged into a desperate state of agitation, despair, and unrestful sleep. He sometimes wishes he were dead but has not had suicidal ideation. He's astonished at the rapidity of his decline, since his life had been going well. He's been taking vacation days, which he has to do in order not to lose them, but is going to work one day a week for the next three weeks. He's been counting on two weeks of vacation in the Dakotas coming up soon. He and Catalina are still together in the same way.

Dr. Sol-Guzman called me after having seen him urgently today. They discussed his going to Stillman, "for fatigue." He and I also discussed it. He actually went on his own to Stillman this afternoon and rested for 30 minutes and felt better. I've agreed to see if Dr. Simmons will open the possibility of a short stay for a medical diagnosis but haven't promised anything. He doesn't want hospitalization, and I think doesn't need it now. It may be that agitation caused by bupropion and atomoxetine could be worsening things.

We agreed he'd stop the atomoxetine and bupropion, and increase his Effexor XR to 300 mg. In addition I urged him to take clonazepam for the agitation and to help sleep. I scheduled an appointment with him tomorrow and gave him my home phone number. I won't be available this weekend but will tell the on-call MHS [Mental Health Service] providers about him.

July 21, 2003
From: Allan Woodcourt
To: Deborah Simmons

Hi Deborah,
Meanwhile, George S. has slipped into a major agitated depression again in the past two days. I've had him stop the Wellbutrin and Strattera and increase his Effexor to 300 mg. I've also had him start Klonopin for agitation and to help sleep. He wishes he were dead sometimes but is not suicidal.

I plan on seeing him every day and letting the weekend people know about him. He would like to have an option to come to Stillman for a very short stay, since he's found that very helpful in the past. I can't put him in for mental health reasons but said I'd ask if you would admit him with some medical diagnoses. I'd follow him of course. He may not need it at all. He did go on his own this afternoon and the nurses let him rest there for 30 min and he felt better. I certainly didn't promise him that you could, or would be willing, to do this, but said I'd ask.

Many thanks,
Al

July 24, 2003
Allan Woodcourt, MD

His improvement has plateaued. Last Thursday he was at "minus

10" and now he's at "minus 4." His usual state is "zero." He hasn't tried modafinil yet. He's determined to leave town for his vacation on August 12. He somewhat resents my wanting him to come see me so frequently, as he's off work now and "it's my time." We agreed he'd come back in a week and be in touch as needed. He'll be resuming with Dr. Sol-Guzman soon.

May 16, 2005
Allan Woodcourt, MD

In the past three days he's sunk into a severe agitated depression. He feels worse than he's ever felt. He paces all day and has trouble sleeping, though he feels exhausted. It's getting harder and harder to eat. He thinks of death but would not kill himself and hasn't been making plans. He wants to go to a "rest house." We agreed that hospitalization would not help because of the environment. He has nobody he can turn to. Catalina is too busy to take time off. He hasn't called her and told her what he's going through. I encouraged him to. He doesn't have faith in the Effexor, though I pointed out that it worked for years and that he's relapsed at least partly because he lowered the dose. We agreed he'd increase to 150 mg immediately. He'll also use lorazepam during the day, which has helped before, and olanzapine at night, for its antidepressant augmenting possibility. He'll be back to me tomorrow, late in the day, and knows about the availability of AHUCC, the university after-hours clinic.

May 17, 2005
Allan Woodcourt, MD

He feels slightly less desperate. He slept soundly with the olanzapine and lorazepam and felt somewhat sedated today, though he was able to get through his tutorial meeting this afternoon. He hasn't taken lorazepam during the day today. He still feels quite hopeless and is sure that his ability to write will never return. He's having a recurrence of his envious obsessions, familiar from prior episodes. We were able to label them as symptoms, at least a bit, and talk about using thought-stopping and attention-shifting. One precipitant, though it's probably more an effect than a cause, is that last week the plans to move his department began to heat up, and new demands on him are coming along. Looking back, the depression was creeping up for perhaps months, indicated mainly by the envious obsessions, which we can now look at as early warning signs.

May 19, 2005
Allan Woodcourt, MD

He's still suffering greatly from hopelessness, and inability to con-centrate. He can't read, or watch television, or write but is going to work every day and getting some things done. He's told colleagues and a few friends, and they are supportive. Two friends will spend time with him this weekend. I briefly suggested partial hospital, but it's too important to him to keep going to work. He's begun to eat, "a few nibbles," and does sleep well. He says the desperate agitation is less.

May 23, 2005
Allan Woodcourt, MD

He's depressed and lethargic. It's not as bad as it was a week ago, but still bad. He's going to work every day and was with friends part of the weekend. He hasn't called Catalina but may do so today. He went back to Dr. Sol-Guzman, and will go again next week, though it isn't certain when she will be able to resume regular sessions with him. He'll reduce the olanzapine from 5 mg to 2.5 mg, and be back to me at the end of the week.

May 27, 2005
Allan Woodcourt, MD

He's had a hard week but says that today the agony was a bit blunted, he thinks probably from the Effexor. Nonetheless, he has a hopeless attitude about the future and feels he'll never recover this time. He's reading bleak statistics about depression, and his own history is viewed in the most negative way. He's seeing Dr. Sol-Guzman on June 1, and one of his friends is looking after him this weekend. He never reduced the olanzapine to 2.5 mg, because he can't split the tablet, but the daytime sedation seems less, so he'll stay on 5 mg for now.

June 2, 2005
From: George Scialabba
To: Allan Woodcourt
Subject: question

Dear Dr. Woodcourt,

I'm feeling no better than last week, and worse in some ways than in previous depressions. Less intense agitation, but also less hope, motivation to persevere, and memory of past pleasures/achievements. I'm almost dangerously pessimistic and worn down. Could this be the dulling effect of the Zyprexa? I know it's hard to pinpoint effect.

George

June 6, 2005
From: Allan Woodcourt
To: George Scialabba

Dear Mr. Scialabba,

This is still most likely the depression which hasn't yet responded, but there would be no harm in stopping the Zyprexa for one night just to see how you felt. What do you mean by "almost dangerously pessimistic . . . "? As we've discussed before, nobody is a good judge of whether their suffering is worse than before. It's characteristic of depression to feel that you've never felt this bad and will never get better.

Best wishes,

Allan Woodcourt

June 9, 2005
Allan Woodcourt, MD

He says that within the last 24 hours the agony is a bit less, but he doesn't trust the feeling. He still has a worm's eye view of himself and his life. It turns out that he won't have to be housed in a corner of his boss's office in the new building but will have a very small office of his own, which is a huge relief. He'll have to come to work on time in the new location. He's not used to that. In his old job, he was able to get the little that needed to be done accomplished on a very flexible schedule. He chides himself for his "immaturity," in that he has a menial job, etc., but at this point, he's still can't say what new freedom more "maturity" would give him.

He found his consultation with Dr. Fjordstrauss helpful, partly because the appointment was longer and "I was able to tell my whole story."

June 15, 2005
Eowyn Trone
Harvard University Mental Health Services

Interim visit set up by Dr. Woodcourt, who is on vacation. Mr. Scialabba reports a recurrence of depression; he's been in a terrible state for the past 5 or 6 weeks, feeling a "tidal wave of agitation." Last night and this morning "about as bad as it gets." He had been taking Effexor 75 mgs as a maintenance dose, but now dose is 450 mgs, and no effect yet. Also taking Zyprexa 2.5 mgs. Having "plenty of negative thoughts." Past treatment with Dr. Sol-Guzman for 1 ½ yrs q o week. Stopped treatment with her and reports her practice is now full. "Biggest mistake I've ever made." Not actively suicidal: "I'm too timid to do it." He has had fantasies of putting stones in his pockets and jumping into the river, like Virginia Woolf, but denies current intention to do so. Appetite down. Lives alone. Still working. No evidence of thought disorder or psychomotor retardation. Not committable. Suggested he consider a partial hospitalization program, as he is in a lot of distress.

June 24, 2005
Eowyn Trone

"A difficult week." Biggest struggle is getting out of bed. He continues to feel some agitation as well, and is using some lorazepam, but not often as he doesn't like the sedation he feels from it. Others have urged him to try a partial hospitalization program, and he's agreed to try. Feeling very hopeless but no plan to harm himself. Makes fair eye contact, no evidence of thought disorder. Affect is sad, speech is slow, quiet. Not irritable or paranoid.

June 29, 2005
Frederick Preston
McLean Hospital

Identifying Data and Chief Complaint:

Mr. Scialabba is a 57 yr old man living alone in Cambridge. "I've been depressed for years."

History of Present Illness:

Mr. Scialabba comes to Partial as a community referral—Eowyn Trone, MS, RNLS—because of concerns of ongoing (5 or 6 weeks) depression. He has had several medication trials without benefit. Agitated, unable to get out of bed. 4 or 5 previous episodes of depression.

Some passive thoughts of suicide w/ no plan. Has been stressed by an upcoming change in his job that requires more responsibility and accountability; fears that he may not be up to it.

Has worked at his present position for 25 years. Describes himself as having great difficulty w/ change—hence this upcoming job change has been unsettling. Also mentioned compulsive book-buying, despite the fact that "I've only read 10% of my books."

Past Psychiatric History:

Dr. Al Woodcourt, Dr. Sol-Guzman

Past Medical History:

Healthy

Family History of Psychiatric Illness:

Mother + father depression

Social/Developmental History:

Born and raised in Boston area. Attended Harvard, major in history. Very involved with a Catholic organization there but lost faith and left. Believes this is where depression and agitation began. Attended Columbia graduate school briefly but dropped out: "Too agitated." Writes book reviews for publication. Has few friends, recent breakup of 3-year relationship. One older brother.

Mental Status Exam:

Mr. Scialabba presents as very depressed and sad. Embarrassed to be here and wary of hospital. Feels he lacks confidence and maturity. Negative thoughts of future, little hope. Denies suicidal ideation—says he is safe. Denies hallucinations, paranoia. Insight and judgment poor.

Initial Treatment Plan:

1) Admit to Partial Hospital Program
2) Symptom/medication assessment
3) Regular attendance

4) CBT to regulate mood/thoughts
5) Return to work

June 29, 2005
K. Applebaum
McLean Hospital

Patient will add walking to his schedule.

June 29, 2005
F. Finn
McLean Hospital

Patient participated in an exercise to identify and restructure cognitive distortions.

June 30, 2005
Dick Purchase
McLean Hospital

Patient attentive to discussion of goal setting process.

June 30, 2005
Maureen Rosen
McLean Hospital

Patient discussed his troubles with depression, which he feels was passed on by parents.

June 30, 2005
Juana Marlo
McLean Hospital

Patient participated in group to identify personality style within relationships. Very actively engaged.

June 30, 2005
Dick Purchase

Patient slept on-and-off throughout group.

July 1, 2005
Maureen Rosen

Patient discussed his ambivalence about continuing in the program.

July 5, 2005
Maureen Rosen
Partial Hospital Program
McLean Hospital

Detachment Note
Mr. Scialabba attended the program for 3 days. Over these days he continued to describe himself as depressed and agitated. He continuously expressed doubt that the program could be helpful to him, that the discussion in the groups was "too simple." On this day he called to inform of decision not to return.

August 4, 2005
Allan Woodcourt, MD

He tells me, with notable anger, that there has been "no progress." He's decided that he has more faith in sertraline since that worked before, so we decided he'd stop the duloxetine and start that. We talked about ECT. He wants me to push him towards that, but I feel that it needs to be his decision. I'm happy to facilitate the process if that's what he wants. He told me that he sees himself as augmenting his own helplessness, partly because his life is so empty of obligations now. The job has no duties, though he goes every day. The move is in late August. He hated the McLean Day Program and won't go back there. I told him an inpatient experience would be like that, only worse. I reminded him that he'd felt better when he was traveling and coping with the demands of that. We talked about his finding some volunteer opportunity that wouldn't involve intellectual work. No new side effects from the lithium.

August 11, 2005
Allan Woodcourt, MD

Once again things are "worse than ever." Yet as we review his functioning, he's quite stable. He won't consider going back to the McLean Day Program. He hates all exercise. I've strongly suggested walks in his neighborhood when the day is a bit cooler. He "forgot" our discussion about volunteer work. He says he's very sleepy during the day. He had already increased his Zoloft to 100 mg, and I suggested he go up to 150 mg. He can use methylphenidate during the day if he wishes. He's tried it before in consideration of ADD issues.

August 18, 2005
Allan Woodcourt, MD

He says things are "worse than ever," but he looks the same and is going to work every day. Apart from work, he does almost nothing, though he does see friends and took a long walk over the weekend. His Effexor dose is now 150 mg, and he's tapering it. I brought up ECT as a way of speeding up the recovery. He tells me his brother, who would drive him, may be going on vacation, so he'd have to be an inpatient, which as of now is unacceptable to him.

We talked in more detail about the move and the loss of freedom and autonomy it will mean for him. I was able to see emphatically for the first time what the issue is.

The Cuckoo's Nest (2005–2006)

August 23, 2005
Allan Woodcourt, MD
Harvard University Mental Health Services

I've called McLean, which has a two-week wait for ECT. He's on their list, and I've asked him to call Betsy . . . to have her set up an appointment for a medical clearance.

I've also heard from Dr. Shonda Penney at Beth Israel, who says he can probably get him in in a week. He tells me that his brother can drive him to and from ECT treatments, so they can be done on an outpatient basis.

August 26, 2005
Allan Woodcourt, MD

He's as miserable as ever but still going to work and occasionally seeing friends. He's exhausted all the time, and extremely anxious about his work situation. He has moved, and will get an office, at least a temporary one, next week. Then he expects to be hit with a heavy load of clerical work which he's never done before and is certain he won't understand and can't do. He has a consultation arranged with Dr. Penney at BIDMC [Beth Israel Deaconess Medical Center] for ECT. We talked about the possibility of his going on short-term disability, at least during the treatments. He doesn't accept that idea now, but I'd be willing to support him.

August 31, 2005
Allan Woodcourt, MD

He's going to work, and so far the new demands have not been too much for him. Finds it extremely hard to get up in the morning, and after supper, he lies curled up on his bed. I told him as strongly as I could that he needed to change that. He says he likes going to movies and doesn't mind going by himself, so he's assigned to go to movies in the evening. He saw Dr. Penney, who is willing to go ahead with the ECT. He's reluctant because it would mean time off work. I've asked him to go down to his PCP today to get the medical clearance and have said I'd support any request for sick time or short-term disability.

He'll stop the Effexor today. He hasn't yet started the Abilify 15 mg dose because the pharmacy just got it. I gave him a Goldberg depression scale to complete. Hopefully he will do that on a weekly basis.

September 9, 2005
Allan Woodcourt, MD

He saw Catalina over the weekend, and his mother. Catalina is "impatient with me," and "very busy and very successful," which makes him feel worse. He filled out the Goldberg scale and gave himself a 5 (maximally depressed) on every item. This week he'll fill out another one, and a HAM-D [Hamilton Depression Scale]. He's gotten his medical clearance for ECT, and the treatments may begin early next week at the BIDMC.

September 15, 2005
Allan Woodcourt, MD

He's scheduled to start ECT on Sept. 21. Could have started on Sept. 19 but chose to go to work and do class scheduling, since he didn't want to leave it for his boss. He's sometimes not going home right after work but going instead to a university cafeteria or a local restaurant to eat. Hasn't gone to any movies but may do so tonight. Didn't fill out the mood scales, but I said he could do that when and if he wished. Wonders about depression support groups in Cambridge, because he doesn't want to go out to McLean. Referred him to the MDDA web site.

September 21, 2005
Shonda Penney, MD
Beth Israel Deaconess Medical Center

Electroconvulsive Therapy, Treatment #1

I. Subjective/Objective:

I met with him & brother as outpatient. I again discussed with him the ECT benefits & risks, the latter including death, cognitive problems, cardio-pulmonary problems, & others. He understood and agreed.

No suicidal or destructive ideas, intent, plan.

Cognition intact.

II. ECT:

Tolerated the procedure well. By 65 minutes after ECT, he was recovering well, cognitively and physically.

September 23, 2005
Allan Woodcourt, MD

He's had his first ECT treatment. It felt "weird," mostly because of the anesthesia. His mood isn't better. I reassured him that he wouldn't feel better after the first treatment. He thinks he may want me to write a letter to his boss.

October 18, 2005
Allan Woodcourt, MD

He's now had about eight ECT treatments. He's having significant short-term memory problems, and forgot his appointment with Ms. Trone, and also forgot that he had any appointments scheduled with me. His brother called me and we straightened that out. He says the agony is gone, but that he feels "numb" and unmotivated. He's not working now and spends much of his time in bed. He is beginning to read a bit, and we talked about something in the *New York Review of Books*. He says he has little appetite. He's seeing friends, "a bit," but finds it hard with his memory problems. He's not been seeing Dr. Gusstav during the series of ECT and thinks he may not be a good match for him anyway.

October 25, 2005
Allan Woodcourt, MD

He's now had 10 ECT, according to his brother, and will have his 11th on Oct. 28. He definitely feels better but still has little motivation and low concentration. He's eating only a little but looks well. He's reading the magazines which come to the house. I'll call Dr. Penney concerning future plans.

October 27, 2005
From: Shonda Penney
To: Allan Woodcourt

We've been treating George S. 3 times every 2 weeks, rather than 3 times every week, since he has proven very sensitive to the cognitive effects of the treatments, starting with his very 1st treatment. (I assume you're getting my written notes—if not, let me know.) He does seem better, by his own estimation, his brother's, and my own, but he feels that he still has a way to go before getting back to baseline. He's had 10 treatments. Many people by now would be back to baseline, but many would not, so he's still within the expected norm. Staggering the treatments as we have, he seems to be tolerating them well, cognitively. My thought would be to keep going on 10/28, 10/31 and 11/4, and then re-assess. As long as he's still on the upswing, in terms of mood, and tolerating them cognitively, I'm not too concerned about the # of treatments.

November 3, 2005
Allan Woodcourt, MD

He says, for the first time in at least six months, "I'm alright." His mood is definitely better. He's dressed better and even smiles a bit. He still has decreased concentration and motivation, but he's eating better and is doing some socializing. He went to a friend's birthday party last weekend and is going to a concert this weekend. He'll be continuing the ECT treatments twice weekly for now.

November 9, 2005
Allan Woodcourt, MD

His life is "bearable but dull," which sounds to me like an improvement. He's had about 13 ECT treatments so far and is continuing at twice a week at BIDMC. He's having significant short-term memory problems, as in having a hard time remembering that he in fact did not go to the concert he'd told me about last week and can't remember why. When he improves further, he feels he'll be able to pick up his writing where he left off. He's still off work and will remain so for the duration of ECT.

November 17, 2005
Allan Woodcourt, MD

He continues to feel calmer but without much motivation or interest. He's worried about his lack of desire to return to work. He doesn't have to face that yet, though, because he's still getting ECT. He's started an analysis with a therapist recommended by a friend. The clinician's name is Patty Bennett. He's not sure if she's a Blue Cross provider, or if she would accept insurance. He's not sure he can afford to continue with her indefinitely at $125/session).

November 23, 2005
Allan Woodcourt, MD

An old friend came back into his life, and he enjoyed their walk in the woods and visit to a museum. He still feels he has "tar in my veins."

December 1, 2005
Allan Woodcourt, MD

He's to have about six more weeks of ECT. He's continuing to feel slowly better, but still spends a good deal of time watching TV and isn't back to cooking for himself yet. His friends all say he's much better; his voice is stronger, etc. There's some thought about returning to work part-time after the course of ECT is finished. He's continuing in his analytic therapy and finds it very interesting but isn't sure yet whether he can afford to continue it.

December 15, 2005
Allan Woodcourt, MD

He's continuing to improve slowly. He was able to think of presents to buy for everyone, which he didn't think he could. He's ready to try going back to work three hours a day on December 20. He has energy, but it doesn't last, and is still quite absent-minded (lost glasses) and has trouble coming up with people's names. He still isn't writing, but he can imagine the way he used to feel and can imagine writing again someday. He'll be with his brother over the holiday. He continues in his analytic therapy for now.

December 20, 2005
Allan Woodcourt, MD

Yesterday was his first day back at work. He feels a little intimidated by the need for new computer skills. He has very little energy. Difficult to get up, but he's been on time for work yesterday and will be today. He's not eating well; protein powder and shredded wheat, etc. I suggested a nutrition consult, but he knows what to do. I also strongly encouraged daily exercise, since he's been very inactive for months. He has plans to be with his brother over Christmas. He knows the clinic will be closed next week but that the after-hours clinic is always available.

January 5, 2006
Allan Woodcourt, MD

He's feeling much better. Has energy, optimism, concentration. Hopes to start some writing this weekend. He's started a new romantic relationship and finds he has some sexual energy. He's soon to decrease to monthly ECT. He's still finding it hard to learn his new job but is getting lots of support. He may go back full-time as of January 31, but if he needs more time at reduced hours, I'll support that.

February 9, 2006
Allan Woodcourt, MD

He continues to feel well but hasn't started writing yet or been sexually active, which barriers he feels he must cross before he can say he's recovered. However, his mood and optimism are better than they've been in years. His memory isn't quite back to what it was and he had some trouble remembering the details of his medication history. He's learning the new procedures of his job and, fortunately, the temp has stayed on, at least for now. He's very slowly exploring the possibility of a new relationship. His ECT is now monthly. Will stay on Effexor 150 mg until the ECT is over.

March 9, 2006
Allan Woodcourt, MD

Mood fundamentally good, though there was a downturn when his office mate left and he was on his own there for the first time. But now feels he can handle the job. He feels not alive sexually, which seems to be a side effect of the Effexor, so we'll taper the Effexor by 37.5 mg every two weeks and start Zoloft at 50 mg for two weeks, then increase to 100 mg. He's starting to write reviews, slowly, and encouraged by the fact that assignments keep coming in. He continues in weekly therapy.

Orgasms for None (2007–2008)

February 16, 2007, 7:33 p.m.
From: George Scialabba
To: Allan Woodcourt
Subject: Zoloft

I've started to see someone and I'm a little concerned about the effect of Zoloft on my libido. Do you think it would be all right to go down gradually to 100 mg?

February 18, 2007, 11:05 a.m.
From: Allan Woodcourt, MD
To: George Scialabba

I'm extremely reluctant to see you taper the Zoloft, though I can well understand your frustration with the current situation. When I get back to the office, maybe we can brainstorm about what to do.
Best wishes,
Al Woodcourt

February 20, 2007, 1:38 p.m.
From: George Scialabba
To: Allan Woodcourt, MD

OK, maybe you're right. I suppose I shouldn't take any unnecessary risks. Do you feel the same way about 150 mg?

George

February 20, 2007 5:02 p.m.
From: Allan Woodcourt, MD
To: George Scialabba

I doubt that going down to 150 mg would improve your sexual function very much if at all, and it would increase the risk of a relapse, so I wouldn't be in favor of that either.

February 20, 2007, 5:19 p.m.
From: George Scialabba
To: Allan Woodcourt, MD

Ok, better safe than sorry. I'll stay at 200 mg.

March 22, 2007
Allan Woodcourt, MD
Harvard University Mental Health Services

He's feeling well. His relationship continues, and he's tolerating the lack of orgasm. He's working very hard. Enjoys teaching but thinks he won't continue after this semester.

May 24, 2007
Allan Woodcourt, MD

Had a bad night after an office conflict, but that died down and he was helped by talking about it with his therapist. He's still in the relationship, which is going well, though he's not orgasmic. He's decided to keep teaching in the Bennington writing program.

August 27, 2007
Allan Woodcourt, MD

Continues in remission. Still in his relationship, and still non-orgasmic. Asked again about lowering the dose of Zoloft, but I argued against it, in spite of what is a significant drawback for him. He'll be teaching in the Bennington program and still writes reviews, as well as continuing to work at Harvard. He's in his psychoanalytic therapy every other week.

November 20, 2007
Allan Woodcourt, MD

Remission continues. He's still in the relationship and enjoying his work. Enjoys sex but rarely if ever has orgasm. Continues in psychoanalytic therapy every other week. I reminded him of my retirement in September '08.

February 14, 2008
Allan Woodcourt, MD

He continues in remission and accepts the fact that he can't ejaculate on sertraline. The relationship continues, and he's enjoying his teaching and writing. He's in therapy every other week. Still has some memory gaps from his time on ECT. He referred to his medication, therapy, and monitoring by me as "crutches." I reminded him that he has a severe illness that needs continued management.

The Devil's Due (2008)

August 1, 2008, 9:30 a.m.
From: Allan Woodcourt, MD
To: Deborah Simmons, MD
Subject: George S.

We share George Scialabba, who has a history of devastating depressions. He's been well for the past two years, but before that he was nearly dead, and was only rescued by ECT, which he had at the Beth Israel Deaconess Medical Center. He has a therapist whom he sees every other week, and I see him only every 4–6 months. He does well on his sertraline 200 mg, but he's always tempted to cut it back. My role is to point out to him what a big mistake that would be.

He's relied on me for many years at University Health Services, but his relationship to me is ambivalent. He felt very attached to Dr. Cindy Shepard and feels very comfortable with you. I am wondering if you would take over monitoring his Zoloft after I retire? If his depression returns, you'd have to refer him out, and my own thought would be that he should go back to ECT early rather than after many drug trials. I'd be happy to be available to consult about him by email or by phone.

If you don't feel comfortable with this plan, please don't hesitate to say so and I'll hook him up with someone down here before I go.

Thanks for considering,

Al

August 1, 2008, 9:33 a.m.
From: Deborah Simmons, MD
To: Allan Woodcourt, MD

Dear Al,

I think I have an open and thoughtful relationship with him and would be happy to monitor his meds. He is having a sleep study soon since he apparently has sleep apnea.

Deborah

Hospital (2012)

July 6, 2012, 11:15 p.m.
Lenora Giles, LICSW
Harvard University Health Services, After Hours Urgent Care Clinic

Patient called the clinic at 11:15 p.m. Friday evening requesting help for an "emergency." Reports being "seriously depressed, in a tremendous amount of pain." Asked if he felt safe, he replied, "I don't think I would do that, but it can't get much worse."

History of major depression, including ECT. Had recently "foolishly" (his word) began tapering his medication. In the last few days he has felt significantly worse, not sleeping, not eating, in acute "pain and suffering." His initial request was for medication. I recommended he go to Cambridge Hospital, as the most efficient way for him to be evaluated for medication and potentially inpatient. He agreed and was relieved. He asked me to speak with his girlfriend who was with him. She had found him "curled up on the bed, crying."

They will go together to Cambridge ER, she will stay with him and present her observations to the evaluating clinician. They will ask the hospital to call and report the disposition to AHUCC.

July 10, 2012
Additri Phill, MD
Harvard University Mental Health Services

A rocky week. Went to ER at Cambridge Hospital hoping to get something to sleep but ended up in a geriatric hospital in Everett. Was given lorazepam to sleep. Mood is better than last Friday but feels very apprehensive, feels he fell into a snake pit and does not know how to get out of it. Got out hospital today. Poor appearance, weight loss, energy so-so.

Thinks he is depressed because retirement account lost $6–7K. Very concerned about economic security.

July 23, 2012
Joanne Levy, MD
Harvard University Mental Health Services

Chief Complaint:

"I have been feeling very depressed."

History of the Present Illness:

Mr. Scialabba is a 64-year-old self-described writer and academic coordinator at Harvard who has a 30-year history of major depression. He has had at least 5–6 major depressive episodes in his life, the most recent of which started in the spring of this year following a taper of his Zoloft medication from 200 mg to 100 mg daily. He described feeling very irritable a few weeks after starting the taper (which was started by his PCP after patient voiced concern over decreased libido), but that the onset has been somewhat gradual and insidious in general. Patient began seeing Dr. Phill in Behavioral Health in January 2012 and tapered his Zoloft slowly. By June of 2012 he began feeling increasingly depressed. The Zoloft was restarted, but the decline continued. Was hospitalized about 2 weeks ago in Everett (went to Cambridge Health

Alliance ER) for 3 days, where Ativan was started with some effect on sleep and Zoloft was increased further to 100 mg daily. Continues to have anxiety. Last saw Dr. Phill on July 10, 2012, and at that time the Zoloft was increased from 100 mg to 200 mg daily. Patient came in today with a close male friend, John, who feels strongly that the patient cannot wait for his symptoms to improve and was concerned that the patient would be headed towards a severe depression if there was not an urgent intervention. Currently, patient endorses low energy, depressed mood, difficult focusing, poor sleep, and fierce agitation (the latter characteristic of his past episodes). Does not have suicidal thoughts but sometimes wishes he could go to sleep and not wake up. Has many friends here in Boston, who give him hope for the future. Patient does not feel that he needs to be hospitalized. Suggested increasing the Ativan for agitation and continuing to give some time for the increased dosage of Zoloft to take effect. Also discussed ECT, as that has worked in the past, though this clinician feels it is premature to discuss this as patient was maintained on Zoloft for more than 5 years with no recurrence of his depression in the past and he is still in the middle of an upward titration.

Psychiatric History:

At least 5 major depressive episodes in the past with very symptoms often resistant to treatment. No manic episodes or psychotic symptoms. One hospitalization (this month), no suicide attempts, ECT in 2005 (very effective). Past medications have included: Parnate, desipramine, nortriptyline, Effexor XR, Wellbutrin, Adderall, Strattera. Saw Dr. Woodcourt at Harvard University Health Services for many years (1993–2008). Has an outside therapist, an analyst, whom he sees every 2 weeks for the past 5 years, but she is on vacation for a month.

Medical History:

Sleep apnea, benign prostatic hyperplasia, sexual dysfunction.

Social History:

Works as an events coordinator at the Center for Government and

International Studies at Harvard. Has been able to work recently, but in the past has missed several months of work due to depression. Lives alone in Cambridge. Is close to his brother and has two other close friends who check in on him regularly (one of whom is present today with him). Denies having access to any weapons in the home or otherwise. Likes to write and has several published pieces.

Family History:

Both parents reportedly dysthymic, maternal grandmother had ECT, first cousin suicided at age 21.

Detailed Mental Status Exam:

Decently groomed, thin, frail man. Discusses his symptoms and suffering openly.

Treatment Review:

Discussed a goal of decreasing patient's mood symptoms and anxiety from a 8/10 to at least a 5/10 over the next week.

Current Plan:

1. Add a second dose of Ativan in a.m. when anxiety is at its worst (0.5 mg)

2. Follow up again this week (July 27, 2012) to assess if the symptoms have improved due to medication compliance with Zoloft and addition of Ativan dosage. Was instructed to call (during business hours) or go to the nearest emergency room for help if he feels actively suicidal or unsafe at home.

3. Will consider ECT consult if symptoms worsen or if no better in 1–2 weeks.

4. Patient will resume care with assigned clinician Dr. Phill when she returns from vacation.

The One-Eyed Man (2016)

April 21, 2016
Freya Gerth, MD
Psychiatric Admission Note
McLean Hospital

Admission & Historical Info

Chief Psychiatric Complaint:

Mr. Scialabba is a 68-year-old single man with major depressive disorder. No prior suicide attempts or hospitalizations. He is being admitted for inpatient electroconvulsive therapy (ECT) due to significant hopelessness and distress over permanent loss of vision in one eye from glaucoma.

History of Present Problem:

Low mood, anhedonia, agitation, poor sleep, poor energy, low appetite, poor concentration, daytime fatigue, and low motivation. Denies suicidal ideation. No SIB. He feels that the main trigger is his vision loss. "I can't get away from it—every waking moment I'm conscious that I am half-blind." Cannot read easily. No history of psychosis, homicidal ideation, or mania.

Stressors: distress over vision. "I had been looking forward to retirement for decades—it was going to be non-stop reading."

Mental Status Exam:

General: Thin
Dressed in: Clean Clothing
Grooming: Clean but disheveled
Eye Contact: Intermittent
Motor Abnormalities: No abnormalities noted, Decreased Movement
Speech: Normal Rate, Normal Tone, Clearly Articulated, Normal Prosody

Alertness: Alert
Participation: Fair/Cooperative
Mood: Depressed
Affect: Other (euthymic)
Thought processes: Linear, goal-directed
Insight: Poor/Limited
Judgment: Poor
Attention/orientation/memory: Able to assess
Attention: Completes 3-Step Command
Orientation: Intact
Memory: Intact
Memory Tested By: Observation from interview

Inventory of Assets:

Bright/Articulate
Adequate financial support
Social/family support
Committed treaters
Stable living situation
Stable outpatient program
Aftercare supports

Formulation:

Mr. Scialabba is a 68-year-old man with major depressive disorder. He has no prior suicide attempts or hospitalizations. He is being admitted for impatient ECT due to significant hopelessness and neuro-vegetative symptoms subsequent to losing his vision from glaucoma. Diagnostically, he represents an acute risk of suicide given his age, gender, being single, few social supports, and severe mood symptoms. He is protected by his desire to get well and supportive partner and treater.

Provisional Diagnoses:

Axis I: Principal Diagnosis:
Major depression, severe, recurrent

Initial Treatment Plan:

Admit To: ABE unit

Estimated Length of Stay: 5–7 days

Initial Short-Term Goals: Acute stabilization; Ensure safety

Recommended Interventions: Individual Case Management, Group/Milieu Therapy, Pharmacotherapy, Family/Couples evaluation/ treatment

Psychosocial Interventions: Intervention Plan at Admission

Attestation:

I certify that the inpatient psychiatric hospital admission is medically necessary for treatment, which could reasonably be expected to improve the patient's condition, and that all required information is contained in the medical record.

April 21, 2016

Harriet Rosengarten, RN

Initial Nursing Assessment

Identifying Data and Current Presentation/Problems:

68-year-old male presents for admission to AB1N. Approved for ECT by Dr. Seiner. Has had ECT in the past in 2005 and 2012. Currently depressed, isolating at home. Feeling hopeless. Precipitant is glaucoma causing blindness in one eye.

Patient reports that he has had endogenous depression for many years. ECT helped in the past. Believes that this depression is reactive to losing sight in right eye. Feels this has destroyed his life plan after retirement. Patient is a freelance writer and wanted to travel around the country. Feels unable to do this given his loss of eyesight.

Mood is depressed. Sleep was adequate until this week. For the last few days, patient has had broken sleep. Wakes up before dawn and cannot return to sleep. Energy, concentration, and appetite are poor.

Reports anhedonia. Unable to find pleasure in reading and writing as he usually does. Had to give up assignments due to illness. Forced himself to complete one assignment but did not enjoy the work as he usually does.

Retired from his clerical job last year after 35 years at Harvard. Went for regular checkup, reported vision problems with blurring and loss of vision. Given drops and had laser procedure which reduced the pressure in his eye. This did not help with vision loss but went to see glaucoma specialist who diagnosed patient with cataract and loss of sight in the right eye.

Patient writes book reviews, criticisms, and essays. Publishes mostly about national politics and policies. Had a column at the *Globe* in the past. Feels his career is now threatened by his glaucoma.

Patient able to have left eye checked by specialist given the issue with his right eye. Plans to see another physician as current eye doctors dismissed his complaints for a long period of time before being diagnosed with the glaucoma.

Born and raised in East Boston. Lives in Cambridge. Has a significant other who lives in Vermont. She has been supportive. Patient has never married. Has a married brother who lives in the area, but is currently spending the winters in Florida.

April 22, 2016
Lewis Coser
McLean Hospital

Request for Consultation

Type of Consultation Requested:

ECT

Urgency:

    Routine

Patient History:

    MDD

Medications:

    sertraline 200 mg/day; methylphenidate 20 mg/day

Reason for consultation:

    ECT

Requesting Physician's Name:

    Casarella

Consultant:

    Franklin Saft, MD

Note:

68-year-old single white male literary critic by profession, presents with treatment-resistant depression of several weeks' duration, refractory to pharmacotherapy. He has had two prior depressive episodes, which were effectively treated with ECT at the Beth Israel, resulting in 100% remission. His current depression appears to have been precipitated by his having developed glaucoma, with complete blindness in the right eye and partial blindness in the left eye. His depressive symptoms include anhedonia, anorexia, insomnia, LOI, concentration and obsessional rumination. He has been refractory to pharmacotherapy and is starting to feel his life is over. <u>PMH</u> [past medical history]: obstructive sleep apnea.

On interview, he was a fatigued-looking man who nevertheless related in an engaging and insightful manner. He had moderately severe constriction of affect, speech latency, motor retardation, and paucity of speech. He was able to articulate his history in an intelligent and perceptive manner with good recall of detail. He would like to try ECT. ECT is clearly indicated, given past response and severe symptoms. It would be desirable to get sign-off from his ophthalmologist.

Plan:

Commence ECT as soon as cleared by his own ophthalmologist.

McLean Hospital Progress Notes (2016)

April 21, 2016, 10:50 p.m.

Nursing Admission Note

Patient is a 68-year-old male admitted at 8:45 p.m. with a diagnosis of depression in setting of losing sight in his right eye. On admission, patient was calm, cooperative, and lucid. He was given orientation to unit and policies. Person and belongings were searched for contraband by [volunteer] Mental Health Specialist Stephanie.

April 22, 2016, 5:00 a.m.

Patient slept occasionally but was awake most of the night.

April 22, 2016, 4:30 p.m.

Patient presents flat range of affect but is easy to engage. He was visible on unit but didn't go to group; not much interaction with peers on unit. Patient denies any safety issues and will come to staff if that changes.

April 23, 2016, 5:30 a.m.

Patient appeared to fall asleep after 11:45 p.m. Seen awake in bed for a few minutes at 4 a.m. After 4:30 a.m., patient appeared to go back to sleep again without incident.

April 23, 2016, 11:00 a.m.

Patient seems pleasant and easy to engage. Stated that the noise (contractors working on the bathroom in the east wing) and lack of privacy is "unsettling." Said he feels "fragile" but will try to be more social on the unit today. Patient states that he feels safe and denies suicidal or homicidal ideation but will inform staff members if that changes.

April 23, 2016, 8:10 p.m.

Patient presents with sad disposition but brightens at times. Reports moving from feeling "zero percent like himself" to "ten or fifteen percent" since being admitted. Attended the four o'clock walk but finds other groups minimally helpful. Has been selectively social on the unit and attended other outdoor groups.

April 23, 2016, 5:10 a.m.

Patient appeared to have slept throughout the night, waking up once for a bathroom break @ 1:45 a.m.

April 23, 2016, 11:00 a.m.

Nursing Assessment Flowsheet

Level of Consciousness: Alert and Responsive

Gait and Posture: Steady and erect

Motor Activity: Free of excessive movements or hypoactivity

Physical Symptoms: None reported/none observed. Patient denies physical symptoms

Appetite/Intake: Healthy appetite/ate balanced meal

Elimination: No problem with bowel/bladder function

Sleep/Rest: Slept 6–10 hours at night

Energy Level: Sufficient for required/desired ADL's [activities of daily life].

Self-Care Activities: Completes ADL's independently, Understands Hand/Respiratory hygiene practice

Thought Process: Clear, linear thought process

Orientation: Oriented to time/place/person

Suicidal/Homicidal Ideation: Denies SI/HI

Impulse Control: Able to control impulses

Memory/Concentration: Memory intact/able to concentrate

Affect/Mood: Appropriate to situation

Learning Needs: Coping mechanisms and skill management

Stressors: Noise coming from bathroom; lack of privacy on unit

April 25, 2016, 9:55 a.m.

Patient considering TMS [transcranial magnetic stimulation], consult pending.

Patient does not want ECT, which carries some risk of worsening glaucoma. Continue with treatment plan.

April 25, 2016, 11:40 a.m.

Patient makes eye contact, is pleasant and easy to engage upon approach. Patient reports depression as "when I woke up, 8/10, but right now, 6.5/10." Reports anxiety "5/10," (10 = worst), reports increased anxiety re: his TMS treatment consult decision. Patient reports he plans to talk to his treatment team about TMS treatment, and tentative dates. Patient denies SI/HI at this time—"I feel stiflingly safe"—and agrees to come to staff with any changes.

April 25, 2016, 10:05 p.m.

In check-in, patient relates that he believes he is improving and that he is coming to terms with the loss of vision in his right eye. People are saying that it is possible to live with one eye. He is interested in pursuing TMS and feels that if it is indicated, he could start any time between the end of the week and two weeks from now. Has felt supported by friends who he has talked and visited with.

April 25, 2016, 11:46 a.m.

Nursing Assessment Flowsheet

Level of Consciousness: Alert and Responsive

Gait and Posture: Steady and erect

Motor Activity: Free of excessive movements or hyper-activity

Physical Symptoms: None reported/none observed. Patient reports no pain at this time.

Appetite/Intake: Patient reports low appetite, reports "that is normal" for him.

Sleep/Rest: Patient reports broken sleep, at least 6 hours, with sleep aids as requested.

Energy Level: Sufficient for required/desired ADL's; patient reports increased energy today, plans to shower

Thought Process: Clear, Linear

April 27, 2016, 9:45 a.m.

Rounds: Discharge today.

April 27, 2016, 2:30 p.m.

Nursing—Flat affect for much of shift. Appeared more nervous closer to discharge. Reports good mood. Some anxiety reported over next steps and aftercare. Attended no groups prior to discharge. Observed alone @ end of hall reading, also at meals and other activities.

Discharged from unit without incident.

III. Conversation About Depression

CHRISTOPHER LYDON (CL): George, I'm one of those friends of yours who is fascinated by and also grateful for your disclosure of your own clinical notes, the doctors' and professionals' notes on your state of mind, depressed mostly, over the last 30–40 years, mainly because we all live in the neighborhood of depression, our own or somebody else's. And talking about it does seem a constructive step. But I also wonder why you wanted to put these notes on the record, and how you read them, how you would read them as a kind of work of literature.

GEORGE SCIALABBA (GS): They're very far from literature. And they're hardly written or composed at all. They're a very distinct form of writing. They're almost a form of anti-writing. It so happens that my current therapist teaches a course in how to write treatment notes. As we talked about this project of mine, she mentioned that, over the course of her career, 30 or 40 years, the note-writing process has changed drastically. It used to be a freer form, more candid and unhitched, uninhibited. Over time, as medical liability has become more of a concern and as the whole society has become more litigious, doctors have become self-protective, understandably, in a way. They've shifted and limited the focus, not to express what may have struck them or puzzled them, not to set down something in their individual voice, just because that's an aspect of being human and being in contact with humans, but rather simply to give future clinicians, and in particular, emergency-room clinicians, something to work with if a crisis happens. The notes have become much more narrowly defined in their purpose and more guarded.

CL: There's too much diagnostic lingo-bingo. I mean "severe endogenous depression, super-imposed on a schizoid personality." What did the man say? How did he look? What human connection was made? Not to mention, all this incredible list of pills you've taken over the years, yet nobody at the core of this record seems to know what's working, if anything's working. Is anything better than a placebo? It's all a kind of fantasy. This is a story without a plot, without characters, without hope, in a way.

GS: One of the things I have learned in recent years is that the definition of everything, including success in treatment, has been conditioned by the requirements of insurance companies and hospital administrators—the business side of the profession. In order to get paid for service, you need to be able to show the people who are shelling out that it works. And they demand quantitative measures, the equivalent of the corporation's quarterly report. How do you quantify a long conversation in which a patient gradually sees the outlines of his or her life emerging? That may be healing, but if you can't measure it, you can't expect to get paid for it.

CL: George, how are you feeling, really? How are you, really?

GS: Ludwig Wittgenstein's last words were, "Tell my friends I've had a wonderful life." Now, if you read a biography of Wittgenstein or his letters and diaries, you see a man whose sufferings put mine and most other people's in the shade. He suffered excruciating depressions. He didn't say anything frivolous or light-minded his whole life. He weighed every word and spoke from a position of enormous intellectual and philosophical integrity and authority. I think he meant his last words. And they have always served as an illumination to me. It doesn't make my memories any less bitter, but it helps.

CL: The rough outline of your story, as I remember, is that you grew up in East Boston with an Italian accent. You were a sort of affirmative action, working-class Italian kid at Harvard in the 1960s. You were active in Opus Dei, a kind of arch-Catholic cell. And you got deep into it, and then bolted out of it. That seemed to have been a turning point. In what sense?

GS: Well, I'm still figuring that out, but I thought, from age six or seven, that I wanted to be a priest. I became an altar boy. I was very devout. I didn't use the naughty words that the other working-class Italian boys in my neighborhood used. I didn't try to fool around with the girls as they did, eschewed pornography, and just kept myself free of mortal and even venial sins to the extent that I could. I think the reason for that was, in part, because my immediate environment, my home and my neighborhood, were limited, very dull, stifling. My parents were decent people and very conscientious. But my mother never completed grammar school, never read a book as far as I know. My father finished high school, but that's all. He was an intellectually curious man but had no way to pursue it. I think I sensed that there just wasn't enough oxygen in this atmosphere. I thought that becoming a priest would at least be a way of connecting with a cosmopolitan organization, a way of leaving home, and a way of taking out a pretty solid insurance policy for eternity, which I still believed in.

CL: What about Harvard itself, just getting a first-class expansive, liberating education?

GS: Harvard comes along a little later in the story. First, I checked out the local Franciscan seminary. Not much oxygen in that atmosphere, either. I went to high school thinking that I would go the seminary afterward. And then this recruiter came from Harvard as part of their affirmative action outreach in the early '60s and said, "Hey, boys, think about coming here." At the same time, I met Opus Dei, and they said (or at least I heard): "Here's another opportunity to live out universal ideals in the security of a large organization, another totalistic thing to lose yourself in." I joined Opus Dei and went to college, thinking I'd made the best of both worlds. It was a good education, although I wasted a lot of opportunities because I spent a lot of time proselytizing for Opus Dei. There were even some courses which I couldn't take because too many of the books were on the Church's Index of Forbidden Books.

CL: This whole story reminds me of an article a year or two ago, by a marvelous writer and doctor, Siddhartha Mukherjee, the guy who wrote *The Emperor of All Maladies*, about cancer and about the history of defining cancer. What is it, and where does it come from? Is it to be bombarded? Is it to be poisoned? Is it to be cut out? Is it all these evolutions that radiated, et cetera? And then he did a kind of parallel reflection on the history of defining depression. The basic line was: "We don't know what we're talking about. We don't know what this beast is, much less how to treat it with exercise, with prayer, with family, with vitamins, with walking, whatever, or much less all these other combinations of surgeries and radiation and the rest." What is your metaphor for this illness that you've suffered with for a long time now?

GS: I have hit on a metaphor that seems useful to me, even if it doesn't cover all cases. It's the metaphor of the shock absorber. We're all issued shock absorbers, but some of them work better than others, and some lives are full of more shocks and stresses than others. If you have a flimsy shock absorber and you're subjected to unusually heavy stresses, then you crash when it gives out. The shock absorber is the whole emotional/psychological immune system, which is partly a matter of diet and physiological health, partly your network of family, friends, lovers, partly the level of solidarity and security in the society you're lucky or unlucky enough to live in.

CL: What events in the real world do you think it responds to, including love and partnership and family or whether or where you are, income, all manner of affirmations or lack of it in a person's life?

GS: Economic insecurity is an epidemic stress. Since 2008, a lot of middle-aged, laid-off men and women haven't been able to restart their work lives and have plummeted into pretty severe depressions. I know a couple of them. That's a terrible stress. And then there's illness.

CL: ECT for electroconvulsive therapy, shock therapy, how was it presented to you, and why did you choose it in the end?

GS: It was presented as a last resort. In 2005, I had a real corker, the worst depression I've ever had. I don't mean to sound melodramatic, but you know, it's possible to be simultaneously writhing in pain and to look, from the outside, almost totally immobile. I was pacing compulsively, but I was also lying in bed, unable to get up, for long periods. I did make it to work every day, but I did just enough not to get fired. Nothing helped. "ECT sometimes helps. Do you want to try it?" That's really all the doctor said. I did. I'd seen *One Flew over the Cuckoo's Nest*. I had my misgivings.

CL: What's the metaphor? What's happening inside your brain when it takes that charge? It's not chemo, it's not radiation, but it's doing something to the electrons.

GS: It's fifty years old or more, but they're still not sure what it's doing. They say it reboots your emotional circuitry, but if you press them, they shift uneasily from foot to foot. But it works as often or more often than antidepressants, on average, or at least it produces from eight- to ten-point improvements on the Hamilton Diagnostic Scale, which is what "works" means for doctors and insurers. Sometimes it does actually produce dramatic improvements.

CL: I want you to come back to the religious question, because for one thing, I've sort of been there. I know roughly the territory. In your case, though, you were a very virtuous young man who wanted to live a kind of aggressively—or should we say, militantly—Christ-like life, in a disciplined way. And at 20 or 21, in the middle of your Harvard education, you decide, "No, no, that's an illusion. It's all wrong." You've been in flight from it ever since. So many of the clinical notes point to this crucial aspect of your grown-up state of mind.

GS: Before I left Opus Dei and the Church, I thought it was a great gain rather than a great loss. I thought I had discovered the truth about the universe, and that by leaving I would be placing myself in the ranks of a great army of liberation going all the way back to the first modern philosophers and especially the *philosophes* of the Enlightenment. I felt tremendously lucky and proud to be a drop in that great wave of progress and truth. And then, when I actually did it, walked out the door, I discovered that religion had been a kind of drug for me, or a safety net or scaffolding. And the reaction I felt was one of agitation and anxiety. Now I was to be on my own for a time—and possibly eternity, just in case I happened to be wrong. I was terribly frightened. I forgot all of the pride and all of the joy and discovery and so on. It just vanished, evaporated. For decades after that, mostly what I felt was the withdrawal.

CL: I hear that very, very sympathetically. To lose that promise, to lose the cheerful assurance of the catechism that you and I both grew up in—Who made me? God made me. Why did God make me? To know him, love him and serve him in this world, and to be happy with him in the next—that's a pretty nice prospect. When we give that up, we give up something huge. Emerson said, "Belief consists in accepting the affirmations of the soul, unbelief in denying them." It's a painful thing to deny those affirmations and to believe in what we grew up calling the soul. But I'm curious that you haven't in a way found your way back out of childhood into a sophisticated, and maybe in some sense skeptical, but new language of embracing those affirmations of the soul. Not necessarily in a dogmatic religion, or an explicitly personal God, but in something large that means something like it.

GS: Like a lot of people, I suppose, I have a potpourri of ultimate commitments or anchoring beliefs. One of them is the visionary utopianism of John Ruskin, William Morris, Bertrand Russell, and Oscar Wilde, a belief in the abiding solidarity of humankind and the kind of heaven that will make possible. Then there's something very different: the paganism of D. H. Lawrence, which is probably the most convincing philosophy of life that I know. Lawrence said he was a fearfully religious man. And he said, "There is eternity, but it's instantaneous. It's vertical rather than extended. It's the depth of your experience— experience sufficiently deep is our taste of eternity." I wish I could say I'm fearfully religious. I have been diverted into political complaining for the last three and a half decades, just because they've been such a bitter, humiliating, disheartening time to live through politically in the United States. In a happier time, I think I would have tried to follow through Lawrence's and other non-theistic religious people's spiritual intuitions.

CL: What is the D. H. Lawrence belief that you embrace?

GS: Lawrence believed that the universe and the individual soul were pulsing with mysteries from which men and women were perennially distracted by want or greed or dogma. He thought that beauty, graceful physical movement, unself-conscious emotional directness, and a sense, even an inarticulate sense, of connection to the cosmos, however defined—to the sun, to the wilderness, to the rhythms of a craft or the rites of a tribe—are organic necessities of a sane human life. "Man has little needs and deeper needs," he wrote. "We have fallen into the mistake of living from our little needs until we have almost lost our deeper needs in a sort of madness."

CL: That's so beautiful. Does that not fill a great part of the gap that opened up when you left Opus Dei and the Catholicism of your boyhood?

GS: It's an incomplete belief system, but yes, I'd say it's what has replaced Catholicism for me. I'm not completely over the hill and out to pasture. But my life is mostly lived, largely spent. I'm certainly much, much calmer, much more tranquil, though a good deal of that is simple exhaustion. It's exhausting to be depressed. As with any foreign body inside you, you either reject it or you die from it. And I think I've rejected it, but it's taken a deep toll.

CL: We all know depressed people. We've lived with depressed people. We know famous depressed people. Some of them have huge accomplishments, like Beethoven, Winston Churchill and his black dogs of depression. After Robin Williams took his own life, we all thought, "Oh, what might I have said to him?" But the real question for people like you, who can articulate the state they're in, is, what should we know about where you're at? And how should people who love you respond?

GS: One of the things that hurts most about endogenous depression—the kind that isn't clearly the result of some external event—is that you don't really believe that it's ever going to end. You have no idea what caused it, and so you can't imagine what the remedy might be. Friends should tell you: "Look. Eventually everybody gets a little better. Virtually no one is acutely depressed for his or her whole life. It will surely get a little better, and probably a lot better. So hang on."

IV. Tips for the Depressed

The phenomenology of depression is endlessly varied. Some of these tips may be useful to many readers; some to a few; some to none at all. If any of them helps lighten anyone's suffering by a grain, it will have been worth the effort. There is no authority behind any of these suggestions beyond my own long experience of depression and what I've gathered from reading about others'. I don't think any of them are risky, but if you have any doubts, talk them over with partners, friends, caregivers, or fellow sufferers.

Waking Up

For many depressed people—for me when depressed—waking up is the worst moment of the day. Emerging from unconsciousness, you are completely undefended. Sometimes there's an instant of blankness and you wonder: is it gone, am I free? Then the horror seeps or surges back. Whatever strength you've gathered during sleep just seems to have amplified it. You've recharged the battery, but the static is louder than ever.

I don't know what you can do about this, except be prepared for it. And see "Sleep" below.

Getting Out of Bed

A hideous ordeal. Probably the best way is to have an obnoxiously loud alarm clock on the other side of the room. It should have a "snooze" button, in case you crawl back into bed, as you probably will.

At some point, perhaps after the third or fourth snooze, try to slip into the bathroom and splash cold water on your face. You'll know you've decided to stay up when you start shaking all over. Maybe you won't, but I do. Just one semi-voluntary spasm after another for anything from five minutes to an hour. Take deep breaths, stretch, splash more cold water.

Years ago, somewhere or other, I read this advice: "The most important thing a depressed person can do is: Get dressed!" Curiously, it helps. Lying in bed seems like a natural response to agonizing pain, but usually the pain just gets worse. Maybe the few minutes it takes to make the bed, wash up, and put on clothes are enough to break some deadly mental circuit. Try.

Getting from One Room to Another

Usually cannot be done with dignity. You will lurch, shuffle, careen. Your head will hang down, your shoulders hunch, you will be a slumping shambles. And when you get to the next room, you will discover that you forgot something you need in the room you just left.

How to Keep Your House from Becoming a Disaster Area

This is straightforward: you pay someone to do it. Otherwise, forget it. After a while, depression is exhausting beyond words. Vacuuming, dusting, laundry, changing the sheets, washing the dishes, cooking, shopping—together these are as hard as running the Boston Marathon would be for the average out-of-shape non-depressed person. You will forget things, lose things, drop things, spill things, break things, run into things. Don't be mad at yourself—remember, you're being invisibly, silently, savagely tortured. You have a perfect right to let things go a bit.

Water

Don't dehydrate. Drink plenty of water, on a regular schedule. Don't wait till you're thirsty. Your urine should be pale, not vividly colored.

For some reason, being depressed burns up a lot of energy. Of course there's no output—you don't achieve anything—but your metabolism is racing. And you cry. Not enough water and you become slightly feverish and groggy. It's very unpleasant, and it's unnecessary. Fill three or four water bottles at the beginning of the day and put them around your house or workplace, where you can't miss them. In cold weather, make yourself a lot of tea.

Food

Everything is hard when you're depressed, even eating. And besides, you're probably not moving around much, so you don't build up an appetite easily. I always lose a lot of weight when depressed.

To minimize the damage, make a smoothie the first thing every morning. Toss a banana, blueberries, yogurt, almond milk, fruit juice, wheat germ, and protein powder into the blender. (If you can stand it, add a little of some weird-tasting plant-based powder—Perfect Food, Ultimate Meal, lots of others—but don't force yourself.) Then, whatever else you do or don't eat all day, you won't be malnourished.

If it's hard to eat, it's just about impossible to cook, so have a lot of snack food in your fridge. But let it be healthy snack food: hummus, Greek yogurt, cottage cheese, hard-boiled eggs, almond butter, whole-grain crackers, celery, carrots, fruit.

Some people eat compulsively when depressed, for comfort. If you have to, don't fight it. But remember, some healthy things are delicious too. Usually they cost more, but they're worth it. Junk food—candy, cookies, chips, soda—is a kind of drug, and will eventually make you feel worse.

Exercise

It is universally recognized, in fact trumpeted, nowadays that regular exercise is good for your mental health. It is less often acknowledged that for a severely depressed person, vigorous exercise can seem as difficult as running *two* Boston Marathons in a day.

At least walk. Ask your spouse/partner/friends/relatives/hired helpers to drag you outside, or even to the gym. Try for a little aerobic exercise—i.e., something that makes you short of breath—each day.

Mindfulness

Is mindfulness the wisdom of the East finally made appealingly practical for Westerners, or is it just another form of Positive Thinking? I inclined to the latter view until I came across Sam Harris's *Waking Up*. If this aggressively skeptical rationalist has found great value in meditation for wholly secular reasons, then no one else need feel overly fastidious about trying it.

At its worst, the pain of depression obliterates ordinary consciousness, as the pain of terminal cancer is said to do. The pain consumes, annihilates, your awareness of anything else. By teaching you to focus on discrete sensations and tasks, mindfulness practice can help remind you that there is a you beyond the pain. It can help you hold on until the pain recedes—which, unlike the pain of terminal cancer, it will eventually do.

A useful place to begin is *Mindfulness* by Mark Williams and Danny Penman. Also *The Mindful Way Through Depression*, by Williams, Jon Kabat-Zinn, et al.

Acupuncture

It isn't cheap, insurance usually won't pay, and it doesn't help everyone, to say the least. But it helps some people; and unlike nearly all antidepressants, it seems to have no side effects.

Passing the Time

A minimal definition of depression is: the inability to feel plea-sure. As its severity increases, it becomes what William James called "a positive and active anguish, a form of psychical neuralgia wholly unknown to normal life." At the extreme, pleasure and even distraction are impossible. But before that, or after it, popular culture can be a so-lace. *Friday Night Lights* got me through one depression, and (I blush to admit) reruns of *24* and *Sex and the City* through another. There's also *Harry Potter*, Bernard Cornwell's many epics, *Game of Thrones* in print and living color, vast tracts of science fiction (don't miss Kim Stanley Robinson's magnificent *Mars* trilogy), and, on the border of en-tertainment and art, Patrick O'Brian's Aubrey-Maturin novels. There's something for everyone in American popular culture.

Sleep

Sleep medications can be helpful, but only temporarily; in the long term, they can be addictive. Getting some exercise during the day should help. Another thing to try is music. For years now, I've fallen asleep to Renaissance sacred music—that exquisite vocal polyphony that sounds like a choir of angels. Try also, for an hour or half-hour be-fore sleep, sitting quietly (or pacing, if you must) and listening to some soothing music. I'm a classical music fan, so what works for me is Bach, Haydn, Mozart—mostly chamber music, but some orchestral—or ear-lier: lute, viol, and consort music from the 16th and 17th centuries. Something or other will work for you—ask friends with similar tastes for recommendations.

Typically, you will fall asleep without too much difficulty but will awaken during the night or at first light and be unable to fall asleep again. Don't lie awake too long. Get up and pace or listen to music or try to read. It is a hellish time. William Styron in *Darkness Visible* has a pithy sentence about this experience: "The combination of exhaustion with sleeplessness is a rare torture." If only it were rarer.

Strangers

On bad days, you'll look and act like a zombie. Fortunately, most Americans have heard the word "depression" by now—there are, after all, millions of victims—and know that one is supposed to feel sorry for depressed people rather than wary of them. Don't be embarrassed if your voice quavers or your eyes fill with tears. Try to smile: it will put other people at ease, and they'll appreciate your gallantry.

Friends

If you've earned someone's unconditional devotion, for example as a parent, child, spouse, partner, or friend, then you're lucky indeed. But even if not, it's likely that some people, perhaps many, love you and will want to help. They can, very much.

It's primal: when you're hurting badly, you don't want to feel alone and abandoned. You want to be held: literally, if possible; or figuratively, in a web of affection and concern. Ask friends to email, call, or visit regularly: some every day, some every other day, some once or twice a week, depending on how close the friendship. The contact can be brief, but it should be regular. Banalities are fine: "I love you." "Hang on." "How bad is it today?" "It will get better." "Have you eaten?" "I think of you a lot." They can tell you what they're doing and thinking about. Or you can sob. Or you can be silent together.

You can send out bulletins: "Liking that novel you brought me." "Took a walk." Or to especially close friends, simple cries: "Can't get out of bed." "Pain level at minus 9 today." "Oh God!"

Don't hesitate to ask friends for material help: to shop for you, to cook, to drive you to doctor's appointments, to come over and watch television with you, or just be there while you clean the house or do your laundry or pay bills, if you find those things too hard to do by yourself. And a note to friends: ask often. Don't ask only once, or assume that because a depressed person doesn't ask, they wouldn't say yes if you offered. They may simply be unable to ask.

Money

Depression may give you a deeper appreciation of Karl Marx's observations about money as social power. Rich people may or may not be happier than non-rich people, but the quality of their unhappiness is definitely better.

If you're non-rich, it's probably best not to make large discretionary purchases when you're depressed. If you're strongly tempted, or it's a great bargain, at least run it by friends or a therapist. On the other hand, do pamper yourself in small ways: almond milk, the best nut butters, artisanal bread, cheese, and beer, gourmet deli sandwiches, that exquisite scarf or vintage leather jacket. Raid your Amazon "Saved for Later" list.

Try not to miss paying bills. If you can't bring yourself to pay them as they come in, have a little box or basket in which you toss them, and every couple of weeks ask a friend to come over and help you get through them. Or, of course, pay them online.

Drugs

After fifty years, billions of dollars of intensive marketing campaigns, and tens of billions of dollars of profits for pharmaceutical companies, it is still far from clear that antidepressant drugs are any more effective than placebo. The only group of people who have demonstrably benefited from the widespread use of antidepressants are pharmaceutical executives and investors.

Still, many intelligent and honest physicians and scientists believe that they do help some people a great deal. It's definitely worth trying medication if you're badly depressed. Be sure to ask about the possible side effects and investigate them online yourself. In my case, none of the drugs worked spectacularly well. Only a couple had intolerable side effects or made the depression worse. One side effect I wish I'd known about is that the SSRI (selective serotonin re-uptake inhibitors) family of antidepressants, used long-term, may cause anorgasmia. (Look it up—you'll sympathize.) As I have been living, nevertheless, on the cutting edge of the pharmacological wing of depression therapy, here are some personal notes on efficacy and side effects.

Ativan (lorazepam): An anti-anxiety drug, one of a class called "benzodiazepines," from its chemistry. It's very effective at putting you to sleep, but also very habit-forming. Helped me calm down after Prozac.

Buspirone: A somewhat idiosyncratic antidepressant-plus-anti-anxietal, whose supposed mechanism I don't remember. Didn't have much effect on me.

Desipramine: This is a "tricyclic" antidepressant, a term derived from its chemical structure. It made me feel a little sluggish, but I think it worked: I gradually felt better. Very gradually, though.

Effexor (venlafaxine): A SNRI (serotonin-norepinephrine re-uptake inhibitor). Supposedly a double-barreled threat. Hopes were high, and it seemed to work at first. Eventually I fell into a severe depression while on the drug and, for some reason, blamed it on Effexor. Apart from Prozac, the only time a drug actually made me feel worse (though in this case, I'm not so sure it was the drug).

Klonopin (clonazepam): Another benzodiazepine, which I took to help me sleep but didn't find terribly effective.

Lithium: This is more often used for bipolar disease (aka manic-depression). But there's also a long tradition of using it for depression alone. It made me pretty sluggish and didn't help greatly.

Pamelor (nortriptyline): another tricyclic, which we went to after Prozac.

Parnate (tranylcypromine): This is an MAO (monoamine oxidase) inhibitor. I forget exactly why one wants to inhibit monoamine oxidase. These were the first class of antidepressants discovered. They've fallen out of favor because they involve serious (for some people) dietary restrictions: you can't have red wine, sausage, cheese, chocolate, fava beans, and a few other things while taking MAO inhibitors or you may have a stroke.

Prozac (fluoxetine): This was the first of the SSRIs, and it more or less put antidepressants on the map. First, because there was an excitingly plausible theory of how they worked: (1) emotional well-being depends on the smooth functioning of a person's neurons, the cells that relay information around the brain; (2) neuronal transmission is facilitated by chemical substances called *neurotransmitters*: serotonin, norepinephrine, and a few others; (3) sometimes neurons absorb neurotransmitters at too high a rate, so there's not enough left to carry information; (4) if you can prevent (inhibit) this uptake of neurotransmitters, the brain can go back to functioning normally. And second, because there didn't seem to be any side effects at first. Alas, there is a rare but dangerous one: *akathisia*, or intense agitation, which has in some cases (or so it's claimed) driven people to suicide. I did get akathisia from Prozac, but not a severe case, and it subsided quickly when I discontinued the drug. In *Listening to Prozac*, Peter Kramer popularized the phrase "better than well" to describe how Prozac sometimes makes you feel. But when it induces akathisia—restlessness, intense agitation—it's worse than bad.

Ritalin (methylphenidate): This is not an antidepressant but a stimulant, often given for ADHD or (*sub rosa*) to help students stay up all night writing papers or studying for exams. I wasn't depressed at the time but lethargic, and the doctor thought it might give me a boost. It didn't.

Trazodone: a non-benzodiazepine anti-anxiety drug. Not as effective but not as habit-forming.

Valium (diazepam): Still another benzodiazepine. All the benzodiazepines work, if you take enough of them. But if you do that, you can't function very well, and you may get addicted. Just as "air fresheners" don't actually disperse the smell but only cover it over with an even stronger (but less unpleasant) smell, benzodiazepines don't cure your anxiety, they just make you less able to feel it.

Wellbutrin (bupropion): Another idiosyncratic antidepressant, whose mechanism is not well understood. It's often used to supplement other antidepressants, and it's supposed to have a benign side-effect profile—in rare cases, an epileptic seizure. I took it a couple of times because it's supposed to counter the sexual side effects of SSRIs. Alas, I seem to be allergic to it; I broke out in a rash both times.

Zoloft (sertraline): an SSRI, which seemed to work better than anything else to date. I've been on and off it for the last two decades. It would wear off periodically, but at first it seemed to have no side effects. Only much later was it recognized that a large proportion of people who take Zoloft and other SSRIs over a long period find their sexual functioning impaired.

ECT/TMS/Ketamine

Like drugs, electro-convulsive therapy has helped many people over the last several decades. As with drugs, no one knows exactly why. It has been said that we are as far advanced in the understanding of depression at this moment as was the European conquest of the Americas when Columbus first set foot in the Bahamas in 1492. The conquest of depression will undoubtedly be much slower than the conquest of the Americas. Federal funding of depression research is projected to be $406 million in both 2016 and 2017. By contrast, dozens of hedge-fund managers receive more than $1 billion in annual income (on which some of them will pay the same effective tax rate as people earning $55,000, the national median income), and the Pentagon has budgeted $1.5 trillion for the Lockheed-Martin F-35 Lightning II fighter-bomber over the next several decades.

Even now, ECT is a fairly blunt instrument, but when first introduced in the early twentieth century, it was a sledgehammer. For very good reasons, patients were frightened of it. It has become much less arduous over the years: there is far less injury, discomfort, and memory loss. It used to be an ordeal; it is now only a pain in the ass. And it usually helps, sometimes dramatically. If you are in unbearable distress, you should consider it.

Besides being a logistical headache (if you're not an inpatient, you will need a ride two or three days a week, and because you'll usually be at the hospital for three hours or more, your driver will have to give up most of the day), ECT temporarily lowers your alertness and concentration. If you're doing it several times a week, you may not be able to keep working. That could be disastrous for you, financially and career-wise. I was blessed with an enlightened employer and—even more important—a strong union, so I twice got to take a three-month paid medical leave. I don't know what I would have done without them. This is one of many ways in which strong unions are a matter of life and death. There's plenty of data proving that poverty and economic insecurity increase depression and suicide rates. There's also plenty of data showing that the decline of (more accurately, the successful assault on) unions has increased poverty and economic insecurity.

TMS (transcranial magnetic stimulation) is a new and very promising development. A magnetic current is induced within the brain for 20 minutes or so. It's outpatient, with no anesthetic, no memory loss, no other side effects. The disadvantages: statistically it's not as effective as ECT; it's done consecutively every weekday for six weeks; it's not as commonly covered by insurance.

Ketamine, an intriguing drug with psychedelic and anesthetic properties, is the newest thing (along with another new—but also very old—thing, psilocybin) and has produced some dramatic cures. It is expensive and not widely available, but if nothing else works for you, investigate it.

Hospitalization

As we all know, unless you can afford a medical concierge and the most expensive insurance and facilities, the for-profit, private-insurance-based health care system in the United States is somewhere between a headache and a nightmare. Inpatient mental health care is no exception. The quality of life is ultimately defined by insurance companies' concern to avoid liability: they tend to negotiate very strict controls on hospitals, so that whatever happens, you don't hurt yourself or others, at least in any way that could result in a claim against them. The result is a nightmare of "safety" restrictions, intrusive monitoring, and utter lack of privacy. That the food is so horrible, the environment so drab and featureless, and the staff so much like cheerful robots, on the other hand, is probably as much the hospital's fault as the insurance company's.

In general, hospitalization is for those who are helpless or out of control. If you're jumping out of your skin, or conversely, unable even to speak, or if you're actively contemplating suicide, by all means seek admittance. Otherwise, you're probably better off in familiar surroundings.

If you are admitted, try to have friends and family check in frequently—not just with you but also with your doctors, nurses, and attendants. All patients are, in theory, special; but their overworked caregivers sometimes need reminding of that.

Suicide

Nearly every depressed person wants to talk about suicide. Apart from mental-health professionals, hardly any non-depressed people do, except perhaps as a philosophical problem (cf. Albert Camus). Depressed people want to open their hearts, to confess their fears and forbidden urges, to be comforted, reassured, persuaded that life is worth living despite this intolerable, indescribable pain. They want the other person to open his or her heart, not recite from a script. The communion of hearts is healing.

(Speaking of scripts: Mental-health professionals frequently ask severely depressed people over and over: "Are you safe/in any danger of harming yourself?" Eventually this starts sounding to many of us like "Am I (or my institution) safe from legal action if you should harm yourself?" Sometimes it seems as though "Do no harm" has morphed into "Incur no liability." They might, as Robert Lowell once hinted, get more useful answers if they asked: "Suppose you had a little button on the back of your hand, and you could simply press it for a quick, clean, painless death. Would you? Would you ever have?")

What one should tell depressed people, I think—tell them emphatically, authoritatively, over and over, as often as the demon of depression urges despair, which is all the time—is that if they hang on, they will eventually feel better. This is close to a scientific certainty; depressions virtually always end.

That may not be enough. As David Foster Wallace explained in a well-known and terrifyingly graphic passage, a suicidal person is a little like someone who jumps from a burning building. Sometimes the pain cannot be endured another moment; it must *stop now*. If that happens to someone dear to you, then for their sake, apart from all the other good reasons, think deeply about how to lessen the amount of unnecessary suffering in the world.

Whether a world that is unable or unwilling to prevent or heal intolerable pain ought at least to make it a little less harrowing and humiliating for the sufferer to exit, or even to discuss that freely, is a question I'll leave, for now, to others.

In a Burning Building

If waves of agony and despair are rolling through you and over you; if gusts of sobbing shake you for hours; if you're choking, burning up, speechless; if nothing matters except that the pain *stop now* . . . then call someone, anyone, 911.

And shame on the rest of us for letting another human being come to that. Above all, shame on the 1 percent, who by the best scholarly estimates are hiding around nine trillion dollars in offshore tax havens. That money could relieve an awful lot of unnecessary suffering. As certain hardhearted people constantly remind us, it follows from the Second Law of Thermodynamics that there's no such thing as a free lunch. That may be true in the very long run, but now and probably for a long time to come, it's a much harsher, hungrier world than it needs to be.

Recovery

Recovery from a severe depression is gradual. You won't regain your full powers immediately. You'll make a lot of frustrating mistakes, and a lot of ordinary tasks will still seem beyond your strength. Be patient with yourself. Ration your effort, and make plenty of provision for small pleasures.

The poet Sara Teasdale wrote:

For one white, singing hour of peace
Count many a year of strife well lost.

I'm not sure I like those proportions for depression. "Many a year" sounds a little glib to anyone who's known the worst. Still, it's true that even a little happiness is worth a lot of pain.

The stupidest, most exasperating piece of advice commonly offered to suffering people is also the truest and most comforting: time heals. Not always, to be strictly truthful, but almost always.

One more consolation: you might think that so horrible an experience would leave you with a kind of post-traumatic stress disorder, prone to nightmares, haunted, even obsessed, by memories of torment and fears of a recurrence. It doesn't. It takes a toll, of course. But eventually you become yourself again, released into blessed everyday unhappiness.

Acknowledgments

John Summers conceived the article (in *The Baffler* 26) that eventually became this book and then conceived this book. He's been an ideal editor and collaborator.

Christopher Lydon, Boston's celebrated journalist-at-large, invited me onto his excellent podcast (www.radioopensource.org) to talk about depression and then asked all the right questions.

The distinguished literary magazine *Agni* published "Message from Room 101." Thanks to editors Askold Melnyczuk and Sven Birkerts.

Damon Linker of Penn Press was imaginative (reckless?) enough to champion this unlikely book to his colleagues at the press.

No one gets through a severe depression—much less several of them—without a lot of help. Special thanks to my friends Askold, Frank, Maria, and Paula, and my brother, Larry.

I'm not sure whether, and how much, to thank the many psychotherapists and psychopharmacologists who appear (pseudonymously) in this book. They all tried, but depression defeated them.